DOWNERS GROVE PUBLIC LIBRARY

3 1191 00563 0363

W9-CCO-892
DEC 1 1997

CLASSIC COOKING
WITH
PORK

641.664
Mollé Philippe.
Classic cooking with pork

WITHDRAWN
DOWNERS GROVE PUBLIC LIBRARY

Downers Grove Public Library
1050 Curtiss St.
Downers Grove, IL 60515

Keep 7-08   DEMCO

CLASSIC COOKING
WITH
PORK

Over 100 Luscious Ways to
Prepare Today's Lean and Healthy Pork

Recipes by Philippe Mollé

KEY PORTER BOOKS

First published in Quebec by Les Éditions de l'Homme, a division of the Sogides group
Published in Canada in 1997 by Key Porter Books Limited

Copyright © 1996, Les Éditions de l'Homme, a division of the Sogides group

Original French edition made possible through the support of *Le Porc du Québec*

All rights reserved. No part of this work covered by the copyrights hereon may be reproduced or used in any form or by any means—graphic, electronic or mechanical, including photocopying, recording, taping or information storage and retrieval systems—without the prior written permission of the publisher, or in the case of photocopying or other reprographic copying, without a licence from the Canadian Copyright Licensing Agency.

Canadian Cataloguing in Publication Data

Mollé, Philippe
    Classic cooking with pork : over 100 luscious ways to prepare today's lean and healthy pork

Translation of: Le cochon à son meilleur.
Includes index.
ISBN 1-55013-876-6

1. Cookery (Pork).   I. Title.

TX749.5.P67M6413 1997   641.6'64   C97-931065-2

The publisher gratefully acknowledges the support of the Canada Council for the Arts and the Ontario Arts Council for its publishing program.

Photography: Pierre Arpin
Chapter Introduction Photography: Pierre Arpin and Dominique Thibodeau
Styling: Caroline Simon
Translation: Brenda O'Brien

Key Porter Books Limited
70 The Esplanade
Toronto, Ontario
Canada M5E 1R2

Distributed in the United States by Firefly Books

Printed and bound in Canada

97 98 99 00 6 5 4 3 2 1

Contents

Pork Will Never Be the Same Again! 7

Rediscover Delicious Pork! 9

Choosing the Best Wines to
    Accompany Pork Recipes 10

A Brief History of Pork 11

Mouthwatering Pork 12

Cooking Chart 13

1. Cold Dishes 15

Warm Pan-Fried Loin Chops and Tomatoes 16

Mini-Sandwich on French Cheese Bread 19

Small Slices of Cold Roast, with
    Coconut Vinaigrette 20

Pigs' Feet with Spicy Vinaigrette 23

Pork Strips, Cauliflower and Vegetable Salad 24

Lentil Salad with Vegetables and Pork Strips 27

Cold After-School Sandwich 28

Couscous Semolina with Spicy Meatballs 31

2. Easy Dishes 33

Fresh Rosemary Kabobs with
    Grainy Mustard Sauce 34

Kabobs with Sesame Seeds 37

Ham and Sausage Kabobs with Rice 38

Braised Pork Loin Chops with
    Green Flageolet Beans 41

Grilled Chops and Olives 42

Ground Pork Patties with Thyme and Nuts 45

Gratin of Pork Strips and Onions 46

Pork Strips and Swiss Chard 49

Ground Pork and Mozzarella Lasagna 50

Pasta Salad with Mushrooms and Pork Strips 53

Pork Pâté Au Jus 54

Pork Pâté with Apples and Pumpkin 57

Potatoes Stuffed with Pork and Cheddar 58

Lunchtime Ham and Vegetable Salad 61

Cold Roast Pork, Radicchio and Mango Salad 62

Spaghetti with Pork Meat Sauce 65

Curry Coconut Steaks 66

Pork and Mozzarella Pizza 69

Pork Medallions and Ground Pork with
    Roasted Onions 70

3. Recipes for Two 73

Spicy Pork Kabobs with Puff Pastry 74

Marinated Shrimp and Pork Kabobs 77

Chops with Scallops 78

Crisp Herbed Spareribs 81

Pork Cutlets with Avocado and Spinach 82

Pepper-Stuffed Cutlets 85

Tenderloin Stuffed with Peaches 86

Tenderloin Stuffed with Greens and Chives 89

Small Medallions with Sesame Seeds 90

Oven-Baked Spareribs 93

4. For Discriminating Gourmets 95

Blanquette of Pork and Green Apples 96

Rack of Pork with Creamy Garlic 99

Braised Rack of Pork with Pearl Onions
    and Apricots 100

Pork Loin Stuffed with Herbes de Provence 103

Loin Chops with Fiddleheads 104

Cordon Bleu Chops with Demi-Glace Sauce 107

Spareribs with Sun-Dried Tomatoes 108

Tenderloin Medallions with Summer Fruit 111

Roasted Mini-Crown of Pork with
    Cranberry Sauce 112

Fricassée of Pork Kidneys and Mushrooms 115

Sautéed Marinated Pork with Zucchini Balls 116

Ground Pork, Tomato and Gruyère Pie 119

5. Buffets and Receptions 121
Cocktail Meatballs and Plantains.....................122
Pâté de Campagne with Prunes 125
Pork Strips Salad with Avocados and Watercress ...126
Panini with Parmesan and Balsamic Vinegar 129
Cold Roast with Orange-Marinated Cabbage 130
Pork Roast and Bocconcini Sandwiches.............133
Liver Mousse Terrine with Almonds
    and Herbes de Provence 134

6. Old-Fashioned Goodness 137
Pork Hocks and Vegetables............................138
Pork Cubes Casserole with Beer and Celery 141
Braised Pork Chops with Cabbage
    and Dried Apricots 142
Pork Mini-Sausages with Beer and Onions..........145
Old-Fashioned Cretons with Chives 146
Shoulder Roast with Pumpkin
    and Pineapple Sauce 149
Buckwheat Crêpes with Ground Pork
    and Spinach Filling..................................150
Pickled Pork Cubes 153
Smoked Ham En Croûte 154
Country Style Omelette................................157
Pork Shepherd's Pie 158
Sausage Patties with Pink Pepper 161
Breaded Pigs' Feet 162
Old-Fashioned Pigs' Tails 165
Winter Potato and Pork Stew 166
Three-Hour Braised Pork Roast 169
Pork, Cheese and Sun-Dried Tomato Sausages 170
Head Cheese à la Mollé 173
Ham Steaks with Pumpkin
    and Yellow Pepper Sauce...........................174

7. Succulent Stuffings............................177
Pork Chops with Citrus Apricot Stuffing...........178
Small Pasta Shells with Pork Filling 181
Stuffed Liver..182
Paupiettes à la Forestière 185
Pork and Parsley-Stuffed Pumpkin with
    Orange Sauce 186
Ground Pork, Tomato and Herb Pizza 189
Zucchini Blossoms with Ricotta
    and Sun-Dried Tomato Filling.....................190
Pork-Stuffed Vegetables...............................193
Pears Stuffed with Ground Pork 194
Blueberry-Stuffed Pork Roast with Cream Sauce ..197
Yellow and Red Peppers with
    Fresh Thyme Stuffing...............................198

8. International Dishes 201
Caramel Pork Cubes and Chinese Noodles 203
Chinese Stir Fry...204
Fajitas and Salsa 207
Fricassée with Tamari Sauce and Almonds...........208
Chinese-Style Pork Strips 211
Pork Sauté à la Martiniquaise.........................212
Pork Roast with Red Kidney Beans 215
Chinese Pork Won Ton Soup 216
Okra and Baby Vegetable Soup 219
Minestrone with Pork Strips..........................220
Mexican Pork Tacos 223
Roast Pork Slices with Chinese Black Mushrooms...224

Cut Chart 226
Glossary 233
Recipe Index 235

Pork Will Never Be the Same Again!

Today's new lean pork lends its deliciously subtle flavor to these classical dishes interpreted for today's kitchens. Traditional pâtés, stews and mouthwatering entrées join with worldwide pork dishes to form a taste-tempting dish for any occasion. After all, pork *is* the world's most popular meat!

Pork today is a lean meat because of improved genetics and diet. Hogs are fed a healthy diet of grains such as corn, barley and soybeans. The resulting pork is lean, well muscled and very tender. In fact, it is so lean that you will have to change the way you cook pork. One of the "myths of pork" is that it must be cooked to well done. Nothing could be further from the truth! Pork should be cooked only to medium or to 160°F (70°C). You should also cook pork *gently* since high heat will dry it out. And to ensure pork is cooked to perfection serve roasts and chops when the color has just a hint of pink. The pork will be tender and juicy, the flavor will be *dazzling*, the aroma *scintillating*! Your guests will applaud your talent!

Courtesy of the talents of Chef Philippe Mollé, rediscover the charms of pork, as noble a meat as exists, whether it is seasoned with the most ephemeral herbs or the hottest spices. Cooked with vegetables or with fruit, pork is truly versatile, a healthy choice you can serve again and again to family or to the most refined guests for those special meals when you are entertaining. Give in to pork . . . it is irresistible!

Jacques Pomerleau
Executive Director
Canada Pork International

The support of Le Porc du Québec *in producing the original French edition is gratefully acknowledged.*
Many thanks to Jim Vidoczy, Ontario Pork, for reviewing and adapting the text and the recipes found in this book.

Rediscover Delicious Pork!

We yearn for you in galantine form, as sausages, pâté or rillettes. We love you every bit as much whether you're a ham, a roast or a sublime barbecue. You charm the palate with the lightest of touches! Be it as lardoons, chops or kidneys, you bring us endless treasures, and everything you have to offer is simply delectable, simply delicious!

Like me, have you been waiting for the right time to sample pork? That time is now and this is the ideal recipe book to start you off on a fabulous culinary adventure. Using easy and appealing recipes, I've demonstrated that pork is a meat with a wide range of qualities that have been taken for granted for too long.

Whether in hors d'oeuvres, soups, entrées, salads or main dishes, pork is a very appealing choice. Always surprising and remarkably good-tasting — provided it is prepared properly — pork is a true dining delight.

I am particularly proud to present this cookbook and I hope you will have as much pleasure as I did in discovering the recipes and subtle treatments that make pork the centrepiece of special celebrations and everyday meals alike.

Philippe Mollé

Choosing the Best
Wines to Accompany Pork Recipes

Combining wine and pork was quite a challenge: with only this meat as my focus, my task was to suggest a wide variety of wines, suited to a wide range of budgets and meeting a series of basic rules. I must say that such an assignment would have been even more complicated without Philippe Mollé's refreshing cuisine. Rich with imaginative flavor combinations, his recipes inevitably lead to marvelous harmonies.

So we can easily dispense with the old saw that says "White meats — White wines" and create the most delightful combinations imaginable.

Generally, white wine goes well with pork recipes featuring sauces, while rosés are ideal with grilled meats. With fried white meats, sautés or roasts, red wine is ideal, providing it is light, supple and served at a relatively low temperature. If the recipe has a cream sauce, it calls for a more supple wine, one with a hint of acidity to counter the cream's richness.

When the recipe requires it (for example, when it includes a sauce made with mustard or juniper berries) or when your guests are in the mood for a more structured, stronger and generous red wine for whatever reason, a good choice is a more mature wine (from five to ten years old), in its earlier stages of development. Such wines have a more muted color, supple tannins, a subdued acidity and a fullness that makes them more attractive.

Since I consider it essential to comply with the standards of wine service temperatures, in most instances I have included temperature readings.

Wine lovers and gourmets rejoice. To you and your guests, Bon Appétit!

Jacques Orhon

A Brief History of Pork

The history of pork is fascinating and sure to spark interest in the hearts of gourmets. And at the same time, it dispels certain myths and sheds light on certain myths that have persisted for much too long.

Today's pork is the result of a process crossing several breeds. Some have more muscle, others are more resistant to illness, and researchers devoted years to finding the right combination: a strong animal, more muscle than fat, capable of producing flavorful and tender meat.

Other factors played a key role in achieving a superior quality meat: rearing in closed buildings, improvements in hygienic standards, nutritional changes (a diet composed mainly of grains and soymeal), regular veterinary controls and better inspection on all levels of government to ensure quality products.

Since breeding and rearing methods have been modified and improved, it follows that cooking habits should also change. The trichina parasite was eliminated from Canadian breeding operations in 1983, so there is no longer any need to overcook pork to the consistency of leather!

But if you still have doubts about pork cooked only until it's medium (about 160°F [70°C] on a meat thermometer), remember that trichinae are totally destroyed once the meat's internal temperature reaches 140°F (60°C) or through flash-freezing, a process that freezes foods very quickly, found only in industrial operations and impossible at home.

All this is fairly technical information, and it may make you lose sight of the many virtues of pork and the fact that its prime qualities have remained unchanged: pork is a tender meat offering refined flavor and texture. But did you know that pork contains proteins, vitamins and minerals that are essential to a balanced diet? Among other attributes, pork has a higher amount of thiamine than any other meat, and pork liver has twice as much iron as beef liver. In short, pork is a healthy and nutritional meat as well as a gastronomic delight.

Read on to discover the many ways in which you can enjoy pork at its best!

Mouthwatering Pork

The following are the main cuts of pork available from your butcher. If you can't find the cut you want, ask for it. The cuts shown here are grouped according to where they come from on the carcass.

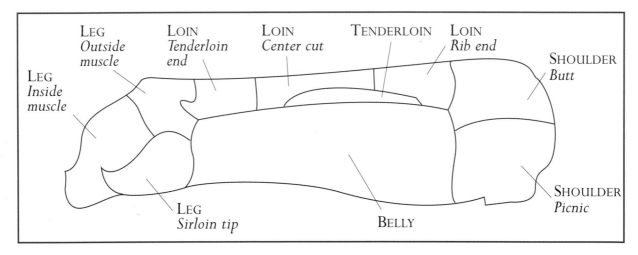

LEG	**LOIN**	**SHOULDER**
Tenderized slices	Loin medallions	Butt medallions
Leg inside cutlets	Stuffed chops	Butt roast/Boston butt
Leg inside steaks	Roasts	Butt chops/Pork steaks
Leg outside roast	Stir fry strips	Picnic roast
Leg tip roast	Boneless chops	
Stir-fry strips	Back ribs	**BELLY**
Stew and kabob cubes	Butterfly chops	Side bacon
Leg medallions	Center-cut loin chops	Stuffed belly roast
Stir fry strips	Rib chops	Salt pork
	Tenderloin chops/Sirloin chops	Side ribs
	Crown roast	Fresh side pork
	Rack of pork roast	
	Country style ribs	

A detailed chart of pork cuts is featured in the appendix of this cookbook.

Cooking Chart

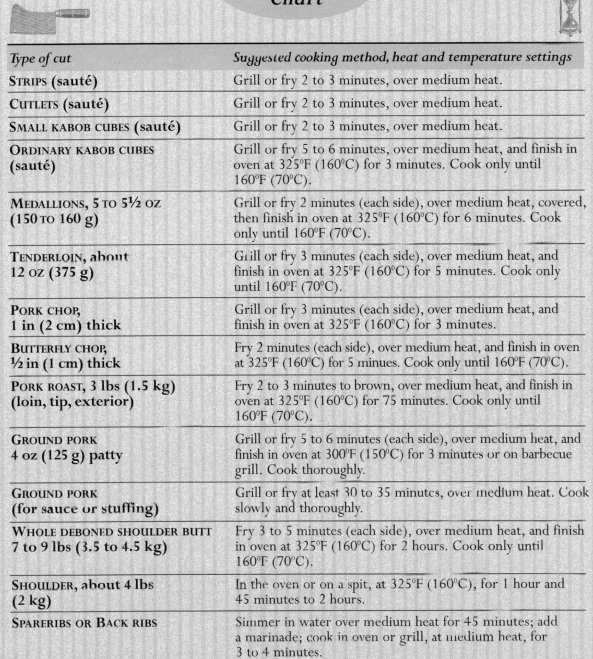

Type of cut	Suggested cooking method, heat and temperature settings
STRIPS (sauté)	Grill or fry 2 to 3 minutes, over medium heat.
CUTLETS (sauté)	Grill or fry 2 to 3 minutes, over medium heat.
SMALL KABOB CUBES (sauté)	Grill or fry 2 to 3 minutes, over medium heat.
ORDINARY KABOB CUBES (sauté)	Grill or fry 5 to 6 minutes, over medium heat, and finish in oven at 325°F (160°C) for 3 minutes. Cook only until 160°F (70°C).
MEDALLIONS, 5 TO 5½ OZ (150 TO 160 g)	Grill or fry 2 minutes (each side), over medium heat, covered, then finish in oven at 325°F (160°C) for 6 minutes. Cook only until 160°F (70°C).
TENDERLOIN, about 12 oz (375 g)	Grill or fry 3 minutes (each side), over medium heat, and finish in oven at 325°F (160°C) for 5 minutes. Cook only until 160°F (70°C).
PORK CHOP, 1 in (2 cm) thick	Grill or fry 3 minutes (each side), over medium heat, and finish in oven at 325°F (160°C) for 3 minutes.
BUTTERFLY CHOP, ½ in (1 cm) thick	Fry 2 minutes (each side), over medium heat, and finish in oven at 325°F (160°C) for 5 minues. Cook only until 160°F (70°C).
PORK ROAST, 3 lbs (1.5 kg) (loin, tip, exterior)	Fry 2 to 3 minutes to brown, over medium heat, and finish in oven at 325°F (160°C) for 75 minutes. Cook only until 160°F (70°C).
GROUND PORK 4 oz (125 g) patty	Grill or fry 5 to 6 minutes (each side), over medium heat, and finish in oven at 300°F (150°C) for 3 minutes or on barbecue grill. Cook thoroughly.
GROUND PORK (for sauce or stuffing)	Grill or fry at least 30 to 35 minutes, over medium heat. Cook slowly and thoroughly.
WHOLE DEBONED SHOULDER BUTT 7 to 9 lbs (3.5 to 4.5 kg)	Fry 3 to 5 minutes (each side), over medium heat, and finish in oven at 325°F (160°C) for 2 hours. Cook only until 160°F (70°C).
SHOULDER, about 4 lbs (2 kg)	In the oven or on a spit, at 325°F (160°C), for 1 hour and 45 minutes to 2 hours.
SPARERIBS OR BACK RIBS	Simmer in water over medium heat for 45 minutes; add a marinade; cook in oven or grill, at medium heat, for 3 to 4 minutes.

Cold Dishes
*H*eartwarming!

Loin, center-cut

or chops

CHEF'S TIP

Keep cooked chops in an airtight storage bag or plastic wrap.

Warm Pan-Fried Loin Chops and Tomatoes

MAKES 4 SERVINGS

4 cooked loin chops, about 6 oz (175 g) each
4 lettuce leaves
¼ cup (50 mL) olive oil
4 tomatoes, quartered
2 tbsp (25 mL) finely chopped, fresh ginger
2 tbsp (25 mL) shredded fresh basil
1 clove garlic, minced
1 tbsp (15 mL) balsamic vinegar
salt and pepper, to taste

Place cooked, warm pork chops on lettuce leaves. Heat half of the olive oil in a pan and sauté tomatoes for 1 minute. Remove from pan immediately and place in a salad bowl. Add ginger, basil, garlic and remaining olive oil. Sprinkle with balsamic vinegar and season with salt and pepper. Place pork chops, tomatoes and juices on a plate or serving dish. Serve immediately.

Mini-Sandwich on French Cheese Bread

MAKES 4 SERVINGS

1 loaf of French cheese bread*
2 tbsp (25 mL) mustard
2 tbsp (25 mL) sour cream
2 tbsp (25 mL) chopped chives
1 tomato, sliced
2 lettuce leaves, shredded
freshly ground pepper, to taste
4 slices cold roast pork (see recipes on pages 169, 215 and 224)
slices of yellow pepper (optional)

Cut the bread into eight pieces; slice each piece in half lengthwise. Mix together mustard, sour cream and chives and spread on bread. Top with tomato slices and shredded lettuce. Top with a small amount of pepper. Cut pork slices in half. Place on bread and top with remaining bread to make sandwich.

*French cheese bread is a small loaf usually made with Gruyère.
You may also use an Italian loaf.*

Leg tip roast,

boneless

CHEF'S TIP

To give a bit of extra color to sandwiches, add small pieces of yellow peppers and leave a few showing from the sides of the sandwich.

* or boneless outside round

Leg tip roast,

boneless

CHEF'S TIP

Fresh coconut milk can be obtained by pressing coconut pulp. It is also available, frozen or canned, in Asian grocery stores.

* or boneless outside round or shoulder

Small Slices of Cold Roast, with Coconut Vinaigrette

MAKES 4 SERVNGS

1 egg yolk
2 tbsp (25 mL) Dijon mustard
2 tbsp (25 mL) olive oil
1 tbsp (15 mL) lime juice
¼ cup (50 mL) fresh, frozen or canned coconut milk
salt and pepper, to taste
½ red pepper, diced
2 green onions, chopped

Garnish
2 coconuts
1 mango, cut into julienne strips
4 whole green onions, trimmed
8 slices of cooked roast pork loin
(see recipes on pages 169, 215 and 224)
1 lime, quartered

Beat the egg yolk with the mustard. Gradually add olive oil and lime juice, finishing with coconut milk. Season with salt and pepper. Add diced red pepper and green onions.

Garnish
Split the coconuts in two; garnish each half with mango strips and chopped green onions. Place roast pork slices drizzled with vinaigrette around each coconut half. Decorate with lime wedges and serve chilled.

Pigs' Feet with Spicy Vinaigrette

MAKES 4 SERVINGS

1 onion	**Vinaigrette**
1 carrot	1 egg yolk
2 sprigs of thyme	3 tbsp (45 mL) hot mustard
2 bay leaves	½ clove garlic, minced
1 celery stick	1 shallot, finely chopped*
3 or 4 cloves	1 tbsp (15 mL) chopped fresh parsley
4 juniper berries	1 tbsp (15 mL) chopped fresh
20 cups (5 L) water	coriander*
salt and pepper, to taste	2 tbsp (25 mL) balsamic vinegar
1 clove garlic, crushed	⅓ cup (75 mL) olive oil
4 pigs' feet, whole	salt and pepper, to taste

Peel onion and carrot, cut into pieces and place in pot. Add thyme, bay leaves, celery, cloves, juniper berries and water. Season with salt and pepper and add garlic. Wash pigs' feet thoroughly, place in pot and cook for about 2 hours and 30 minutes to 3 hours. Keep feet covered with water during cooking. Cool pigs' feet and cut them in half lengthwise.

Vinaigrette
Mix egg yolk and hot mustard. Add minced garlic, shallot, parsley and coriander. Add balsamic vinegar and olive oil. Season with salt and pepper to taste. Dilute vinaigrette with 2 tbsp (25 mL) water, if needed.

Place pigs' feet in a serving dish and drizzle with vinaigrette. Garnish with sliced onions.

* See glossary

Feet

CHEF'S TIP

Pigs' feet are more popular in some parts of the world than in others. Use them when making bouillons. They are excellent in broths because of their high gelatin content.

Strips

CHEF'S TIP

Be careful not to overcook strips when stir frying or they will become tough. An alternative method is to cook them on the barbecue for 3 to 4 minutes.

Pork Strips, Cauliflower and Vegetable Salad

MAKES 4 SERVINGS

3 tbsp (45 mL) olive oil
½ lb (250 g) pork strips, cut from leg or loin
1 cauliflower, cut in flowerets, blanched
1 yellow pepper, sliced
salt and pepper, to taste
1 clove garlic, minced
½ cup (125 mL) dry white wine
2 tbsp (25 mL) balsamic vinegar
2 tbsp (25 mL) chopped fresh parsley
2 tomatoes, sliced
1 tsp (5 mL) saffron, spigol or paprika

Heat olive oil and cook strips, cut in half widthwise, for 2 to 3 minutes. Add cauliflower, yellow pepper and cook for about 2 more minutes. Season with salt and pepper. Add garlic, white wine, cover and cook for 3 minutes. Remove from heat and let cool. Add balsamic vinegar and parsley. Stir, add tomato slices. Sprinkle with saffron, spigol or paprika for color. Keep refrigerated before serving.

Spigol is a less expensive derivative of saffron. It is available in grocery stores and gourmet shops.

Lentil Salad with Vegetables and Pork Strips

MAKES 4 SERVINGS

1 cup (250 mL) green lentils
1 lb (500 g) pork strips, cut from leg or loin
2 tbsp (25 mL) soy sauce
3 tbsp (45 mL) vegetable oil
8 courgettes or small zucchinis
1 onion, chopped
1 clove garlic, finely minced
4 tbsp (50 mL) olive oil
3 tbsp (45 mL) chopped fresh coriander*
salt and pepper, to taste
4 red leaf lettuce leaves
1 cup (250 mL) green beans, trimmed and rinsed

Cook lentils in salted water for 30 to 45 minutes, over medium heat. Drain and rinse lentils. Set aside. Marinate pork strips for 30 minutes in soy sauce and vegetable oil. Sauté pork strips and zucchinis for 4 to 5 minutes. Remove from heat and let cool.

In a large bowl, combine lentils, onion, garlic, olive oil, coriander, salt and pepper. Place on the red lettuce leaves and add pork strips and green beans.

* See glossary

Strips

CHEF'S TIP

To facilitate digestion, you can soak lentils in cold water ahead of time, for 1 hour to 1 hour and 30 minutes.

Lentils and pork are excellent sources of iron.

CHEF'S TIP

*Thin slices are best when
serving pork
to children or making
sandwiches.*

Cold After-School Sandwich

MAKES 2 SERVINGS

2 kaiser rolls
2 tbsp (25 mL) mayonnaise
1 tbsp (15 mL) chopped pickles
1 tbsp (15 mL) hot mustard
2 lettuce leaves
2 slices Gruyère, Swiss or havarti cheese
4 slices of cooked pork roast (see recipes on pages 169, 215 and 224)
1 tomato, sliced thin
grilled zucchini slices (optional)
salt and pepper, to taste

Cut rolls in half. Mix together mayonnaise, pickles and mustard and spread generously on rolls. Add lettuce, cheese, pork and tomato, and zucchini slices, if desired. Season sparingly with salt and pepper and serve.

* or loin roast

Couscous Semolina with Spicy Meatballs

1 lb (500 g) lean ground pork
3 tbsp (45 mL) fresh coriander*, chopped
1 tsp (5 mL) Worcestershire sauce
2 tbsp (25 mL) ketchup or chili sauce
1 egg
2 tbsp (25 mL) chopped raisins
1 clove garlic, minced
salt and pepper, to taste
2 tbsp (25 mL) olive oil
1 cup (250 mL) couscous semolina or bulgur
2 cups (500 mL) water
2 tbsp (25 mL) butter
18 whole almonds

Mix together pork, half the coriander, Worcestershire sauce, ketchup or chili sauce, egg, chopped raisins and garlic. Season with salt and pepper. Shape meat into balls about the size of walnuts. In a large skillet, heat olive oil and cook meatballs for 2 to 3 minutes. Set aside. Place semolina or bulgur in an ovenproof dish, then heat water and butter. Pour boiling water over semolina or bulgur and cook in oven at 300°F (150°C) for 15 minutes. Place meatballs and whole almonds on top. Cook an additional 2 to 3 minutes and sprinkle with fresh coriander.

* See glossary

Ground pork

CHEF'S TIP

You can also add Gruyère-type cheese or cheddar to this recipe or, better still, try it with goat's milk cheese.

WINE SUGGESTIONS

Fairly full-bodied red wines with a relatively high tannin content and a straightforward taste structure will stand up well to the rich flavors in this recipe. Choose between a young Cahors with rustic notes, a dark-colored Coteaux du Languedoc or a Fitou worthy of the name.

Easy Dishes

Ready, set, go!

Cubes for kabobs

CHEF'S TIP

Pork cubes for kabobs can be marinated in wine or in a variety of flavored liquids. Make sure to dry them thoroughly before cooking.

WINE SUGGESTIONS

Despite the subtle seasonings in the creamy sauce, these brochettes are packed with flavor and delicious with light red wines served chilled 55°F (13°C). Try Valpolicella or, better still, Sancerre wines (Loire Valley) and wines from the Alsace region (tender and fruity reds with a Pinot Noir base).

Fresh Rosemary Kabobs with Grainy Mustard Sauce

MAKES 4 SERVINGS

1 lb (500 g) pork loin or leg cut into ¾ in (2 cm) cubes
2 small zucchinis, in chunks
1 red pepper, cut in large pieces
3 tbsp (45 mL) olive oil
salt and pepper, to taste
1 tbsp (15 mL) fresh rosemary*

Sauce
½ cup (125 mL) whipping cream (35%)
½ clove garlic, finely minced
1 tomato, seeded and cut into strips
salt and pepper, to taste
3 tbsp (45 mL) grainy mustard

Alternate pork cubes, zucchinis and peppers on skewers. Brush with olive oil. Season with salt and pepper and cook on barbecue for 6 to 8 minutes. Sprinkle with rosemary.

Sauce
Heat cream, garlic and tomato. Season with salt and pepper. Cook 2 to 3 minutes. Add mustard, bring to a boil and serve separately.

* See Fresh herbs in glossary

Kabobs with Sesame Seeds

MAKES 4 SERVINGS

1 lb (500 g) pork loin cubes
2 tbsp (25 mL) vegetable oil
3 tbsp (45 mL) soy sauce
2 tbsp (25 mL) honey
1 tsp (5 mL) minced garlic
½ tsp (2 mL) ground coriander
½ tsp (2 mL) Tabasco sauce
salt and pepper, to taste
1 tbsp (15 mL) chopped fresh parsley
2 tbsp (25 mL) sesame seeds

Cut brochette cubes in half or flatten them to ¾ in (1.5 cm) thickness, then thread on skewers in groups of three. Preheat cast iron frying pan, brush brochettes with vegetable oil and fry for 2 to 3 minutes. Mix together soy sauce, honey, garlic, coriander, Tabasco sauce, salt, pepper and parsley and brush meat with mixture during cooking. Sprinkle with sesame seeds, turn kabobs and continue cooking for 3 to 4 minutes longer. Baste again with sauce, cover and let rest for 2 to 3 minutes.

Cubes for kabobs

CHEF'S TIP

Use chopped peanuts or pecans instead of sesame seeds.

WINE SUGGESTIONS

With these brochettes, ideal choices are vibrant and refreshing reds with a slightly spicy note, lots of fruity flavor and vigor to spare, such as Costières de Nîmes and other Coteaux du Tricastin (Southeast France) wines.

Ham

WINE SUGGESTIONS

The wonderful flavors in this recipe can be enhanced with supple red or rosé wines, as long as they boast a strong structure. Minervois and Saint-Chinian wines (Languedoc reds), served at 59°F (16°C), or well chilled Spanish rosés (Penedés or Rioja are good examples).

Ham and Sausage Kabobs with Rice

MAKES 4 SERVINGS

⅓ cup (75 mL) maple syrup
2 tbsp (25 mL) soy sauce
½ tsp (2 mL) ground coriander
1 lb (500 g) precooked ham cubes
4 pork sausages
2 peaches or apricots, cut into chunks
1 green pepper, cut into chunks
1 cup (250 mL) white rice
1 onion, chopped
½ yellow pepper, cut into julienne strips
1 tomato, seeded and cut into julienne strips
3 cups (750 mL) chicken bouillon
½ tsp (2 mL) mild paprika
salt and pepper, to taste

Mix together maple syrup, soy sauce and coriander. Add ham cubes and marinate in mixture for 30 minutes. Pierce sausages with a toothpick and blanch* for 2 to 3 minutes. Place sausages in an ovenproof dish or pan and bake in a 275°F (140°C) oven for 15 minutes. Alternately thread ham cubes, peach or apricot pieces and green pepper pieces on skewers and cover; bake kabobs at 225°F (110°C) for 4 to 5 minutes. Brush often with marinade.

Combine rice, onion, yellow pepper, tomato, bouillon and paprika in a casserole dish. Place in oven and cook, covered, for 20 to 25 minutes. Remove cover and place brochettes on top; cook an additional 4 to 5 minutes. Season with salt and pepper, if desired. Sausages can be added at the same time for reheating; recipe can be served in a terrine or ceramic dish.

* See glossary

Braised Pork Loin Chops with Green Flageolet Beans

MAKES 2 SERVINGS

3 tbsp (45 mL) unsalted butter
2 boneless pork loin chops, 2 in (5 cm) thick
2 onions, sliced
1 bottle of beer
salt and pepper
3 tbsp (45 mL) brown veal stock*
14 oz (400 mL) green flageolet** beans, cooked
½ clove garlic, minced
black pepper, freshly ground, to taste

Melt butter in pan and cook pork chops for 1 to 2 minutes on each side. Remove pork chops and set aside. In the same pan, sauté onions for 3 to 4 minutes, until tender. Place onions in ovenproof dish and add chops. Add beer, salt and pepper and bake in oven at 325°F (160°C) for 5 to 7 minutes. Remove chops and cover with aluminum foil to keep warm. Deglaze cooking dish with veal stock. Thicken over low heat, stirring constantly. Strain sauce. Rinse beans in running water. Reheat beans in cooking dish with garlic and freshly ground pepper for 3 to 4 minutes, over low heat. Place beans in serving dish or individual plates. Split chops, butterfly-style, and place over beans. Coat with sauce.

*You may substitute canned beef broth or bouillon
** See glossary*

Loin, center-cut

or chops

CHEF'S TIP

For best results, to prevent a crust from forming do not sear chops too quickly.

WINE SUGGESTIONS

This delicious dish is the perfect match for a dry and supple white wine with a simple taste structure but a fair amount of acidity. A slightly woody Chardonnay produced in Chile, a Soave Classico (Veneto) or an Alsace Pinot Blanc would be delicious, served at between 46 and 50°F (8 and 10°C).

Loin, center-cut

or chops

CHEF'S TIP

Baby squash, which belongs to the squash and courgette family, is easy to find in the summer and fall at farmers' markets or in grocery stores. If baby squash isn't available, use courgettes instead.

WINE SUGGESTIONS

Make your meal colorful by choosing a dry, fruity rosé vigorous enough to highlight the Mediterranean flavors featured in this dish. Try a Rioja rosé (Spain), a Corbières rosé (Languedoc) or, better yet, a Tavel (Rhône Valley), served chilled (46°F/8°C).

Grilled Chops and Olives

MAKES 4 SERVINGS

45 mL (3 tbsp) vegetable oil
2 shallots*, finely chopped
1 tomato, seeded and finely diced
1 red pepper, cut into julienne strips
salt and pepper, to taste
½ cup (125 mL) dry white wine
⅓ cup (75 mL) beef broth
½ cup (125 mL) green and black olives, mixed
2 tbsp (25 mL) chopped chives
enough oil to brush chops
4 chops, 1½ in (4 cm) thick

Garnish
1 cup (250 mL) baby squash, courgettes (zucchinis) or squash
herbs of your choice, to taste

In a pan, heat vegetable oil and sauté — but do not brown — shallots, tomato and red pepper for 2 to 3 minutes. Season lightly with salt and pepper. Add white wine and reduce liquid to three-quarters of original amount. Add broth. Blanch olives in boiling water for 1 to 2 minutes to remove salt. Add olives to sauce. Cook for 2 to 3 minutes. Add chives and set sauce aside. Brush chops lightly with oil, season with salt and pepper and grill in pan for 2 to 3 minutes on each side. Finish cooking chops in oven, at 325°F (160°C) for 3 minutes.

Garnish
Remove tips from baby squash, courgettes or squash and sauté in pan with herbs for 2 to 3 minutes.

Place sauce, olives and garnish on individual plates and add pork chops.

* See glossary

Ground Pork Patties with Thyme and Nuts

MAKES 4 SERVINGS

⅓ cup (75 mL) mixed nuts, unsalted
½ tsp (2 mL) chopped fresh thyme
1 onion, chopped
1 egg
3 tbsp (45 mL) chili sauce
1 tbsp (15 mL) Worcestershire sauce
1 lb (500 g) lean ground pork
½ cup (125 mL) chopped, cooked mushrooms
salt and pepper, to taste
3 tbsp (45 mL) vegetable oil

Garnish
2 tbsp (25 mL) vegetable oil
4 potatoes, sliced
1 cauliflower, blanched
fresh or dried herbs, to taste (optional)

Mix together nuts, thyme, onion, egg, chili sauce and Worcestershire sauce. Gradually add ground pork and mushrooms. Season with salt and pepper. Shape mixture into patties and fry in oil, in a nonstick pan, for 4 to 5 minutes on each side. Finish cooking patties in oven for 4 to 5 minutes, at 350°F (180°C).

Garnish
Heat oil in pan and sauté potato slices and blanched cauliflower for 4 to 5 minutes. Add fresh or dried herbs to taste, if desired. Place patties and vegetables of your choice on a serving dish or on individual plates. Patties can be served as is or with a mustard or tomato sauce.

Ground pork

CHEF'S TIP

This dish can also be prepared with other herbs such as oregano or sage.

WINE SUGGESTIONS

Rosé wines are excellent with these pork patties, given the spicy note created by the chili sauce. Rosés from Italy, Spain or the South of France, dry and vigorous, with a slight bite, are excellent choices and should be served well chilled.

CHEF'S TIP

*Curry is a mixture of spices.
It comes in different colors,
from red to green.*

WINE SUGGESTIONS

*It isn't always easy to find
a wine that goes well with
onions! A well-chilled
Sylvaner, commonly served
with the delicious onion
tarts of Alsace, has just
the right simple and fruity
taste to accompany this dish
marvelously well.*

Gratin of Pork Strips and Onions

MAKES 4 SERVINGS

1 lb (500 g) pork strips cut from leg or loin
2 onions, sliced
1 clove garlic, minced
¾ cup (175 mL) dry white wine
2 tbsp (25 mL) mild paprika
1 tbsp (15 mL) curry powder
½ tsp (2 mL) ground ginger
¼ tsp (1 mL) ground cinnamon
salt and pepper, to taste
1 tbsp (15 mL) coriander* or parsley, chopped

Mix together pork strips and all other ingredients except coriander or parsley. Season with salt and pepper and marinate for 20 to 30 minutes in refrigerator. Fill small gratin dishes with mixture. Cook in oven at 300°F (150°C) for 30 minutes. Increase oven temperature to 350 or 375°F (180 or 190°C) and continue cooking for about 3 to 4 minutes. Remove from oven, let stand for 2 minutes and sprinkle with coriander or parsley.

* See glossary

Pork Strips and Swiss Chard

MAKES 4 SERVINGS

1 bunch of Swiss chard
3 tbsp (45 mL) vegetable oil
1 lb (500 g) pork strips cut from loin or leg
3 tbsp (45 mL) tamari* sauce
1 tbsp (15 mL) grated ginger
½ cup (125 mL) beef broth
salt and pepper, to taste
6 basil leaves, chopped, to taste (optional)

Separate Swiss chard leaves from stems and shred coarsely. Cut Swiss chard ribs into slices 2 in (5 cm) thick. In a pan, heat vegetable oil and cook pork strips for 2 to 3 minutes; set aside. Blanch Swiss chard slices in salted boiling water and strain. Add to pork strips. Add tamari sauce, ginger, beef broth, salt and pepper. Add shredded Swiss chard leaves and cook, covered, for 2 to 3 minutes. Add chopped basil leaves, if desired. Serve immediately.

This recipe can also be prepared with celery.

* See glossary

Strips

CHEF'S TIP

Swiss chard, relatively unfamiliar to most cooks, can be used like celery. It is delicious braised or steamed.

WINE SUGGESTIONS

For this straight forword recipe, a simple white wine is the best choice, especially since it's fairly hard to find a wine that combines well with Swiss chard or celery (whichever you happen to be using). Orvieto (Umbria), Côtes de Duras (Southwest France) and other Picpoul de Pinet wines (Coteaux du Languedoc) should be served well chilled (46°F / 8°C).

Ground pork

CHEF'S TIP

Mozzarella is a mild white cheese that is referred to as bocconcini when it isn't aged.

WINE SUGGESTIONS

A salute to Italy, this dish begs to be served with full-bodied, fruity red wines. The choice is yours: Sangiovese de Romagna (Émilie-Romagne), Rosso di Montalcino (Tuscany) or Torgiano rosso (Umbria). Serve chilled (60 to 64°F / 16 to 18°C).

Ground Pork and Mozzarella Lasagna

MAKES 6 SERVINGS

3 tbsp (45 mL) olive oil
1 onion, chopped
1 lb (500 g) lean ground pork
1 tsp (5 mL) oregano
2 cloves garlic, minced
1 tbsp (15 mL) basil
¼ cup (50 mL) chili sauce
salt and pepper, to taste
1 package rippled lasagna noodles, 1 lb (500 g)
2 tbsp (25 mL) butter
1 cup (250 mL) béchamel sauce*
1 cup (250 mL) tomato sauce
6 slices mozzarella

Heat olive oil in pan and cook onion for 3 to 4 minutes. Add ground pork, oregano, garlic and basil and cook for 5 to 6 minutes. Add chili sauce, mix in thoroughly, season with salt and pepper and cook, covered, for 3 to 4 minutes. Let mixture cool.

Blanch lasagna noodles in salted water. Butter 9 x 13 in (23 x 33 cm) dish. Layer lasagna noodles, béchamel sauce, meat mixture and tomato sauce, ending with lasagna noodles. Top with cheese and bake in oven for 30 to 35 minutes, at 300°F (150°C).

🐚 *Precooked lasagna noodles do not require blanching and can be used as is.*

* See glossary

Pasta Salad with Mushrooms and Pork Strips

MAKES 4 SERVINGS

3 tbsp (45 mL) butter
1 lb (500 g) pork strips cut from leg or loin
½ lb (250 g) mushrooms, quartered
salt and pepper, to taste
4 cups (1 L) beef broth
1 cup (250 mL) water
½ lb (250 g) pasta (penne, rotini, shells, etc.)
½ tsp (2 mL) nutmeg
1 clove garlic, minced
¼ cup (50 mL) whipping cream (35%)
3 tbsp (45 mL) grated Parmesan
2 tbsp (25 mL) chopped fresh parsley
½ tsp (2 mL) paprika

Melt butter in skillet and brown pork strips and mushrooms for 2 to 3 minutes, until tender. Season with salt and pepper. Add beef broth and water and bring to a boil; add pasta. Add nutmeg and garlic, stir well. Cook for 15 to 20 minutes, stirring constantly. Add cream and Parmesan 2 to 3 minutes before cooking is completed. Sprinkle with parsley and paprika.

The pasta cooks in the beef broth.

Strips

CHEF'S TIP

Strips usually come from the leg or loin.

WINE SUGGESTIONS

This is a succulent dish, perfect for anyone who loves Italian food. Choose a delicate Franciacorta Bianco (Lombardy) or an excellent Vino da Tavola produced in Piedmont or Tuscany, with a Chardonnay grape base. Serve at 50°F (10°C).

Ground pork

CHEF'S TIP

For pâtés, it's best to grind your own meat and to be sure not to grind too finely.

WINE SUGGESTIONS

Fruity, zesty whites, such as Sylvaner or Riesling wines from Alsace and Germany (choose dry wines) and certain dry and light rosés (to set off the rich red tomatoes) get along just fine with this pâté.

Pork Pâté Au Jus

MAKES 6 SERVINGS

1 lb (500 g) ground pork
3 tbsp (45 mL) thinly sliced onion
2 tbsp (25 mL) chopped fresh parsley
2 cloves garlic, minced
1 can of tomatoes, 28 oz (796 mL), with juice
2 whole eggs
½ tsp (2 mL) nutmeg
½ tsp (2 mL) cloves
1 tbsp (15 mL) grated fresh ginger
salt and pepper, to taste
4 cabbage leaves

In a large dish, blend together ground pork, onion, parsley, garlic, crushed tomatoes with juice, eggs, nutmeg, cloves and ginger. Season with salt and pepper. Blanch cabbage leaves in boiling salted water for 1 minute. Let cool. Place meat mixture in terrine and cover with blanched cabbage leaves. Cook pâté in a bain-marie* for 1 hour and 15 minutes to 1 hour and 30 minutes, in a 325°F (160°C) oven. Let pâté come to room temperature before serving. This dish can be served with potatoes, mixed vegetables or rice.

* See glossary

Pork Pâté with Apples and Pumpkin

MAKES 6 TO 8 SERVINGS

1 lb (500 g) pieces of pork from shoulder
1 onion, cut into pieces
4 apples, peeled and cored
3 tbsp (45 mL) parsley
1 clove garlic
½ cup (125 mL) pumpkin
2 eggs
3 tbsp (45 mL) gin
½ tsp (2 mL) whole cloves
½ tsp (2 mL) ground cinnamon
½ tsp (2 mL) nutmeg
salt and pepper, to taste

Using a food processor or meat grinder, grind pork cubes, onion, apples, parsley, garlic and pumpkin. Mix together with eggs, gin and spices. Spoon mixture into a terrine. Season with salt and pepper. Cook in a bain-marie* for 1 hour to 1 hour 30 minutes, in a 350°F (180°C) oven. Remove from bain-marie and let cool.

Serve with an apple, pumpkin or tomato sauce flavored with celery.

𝒞 *For this dish, grind pork coarsely; meat should not resemble regular ground pork.*

* See glossary

Shoulder pieces

CHEF'S TIP

For a smoother pâté, use meat cut from the jowl or belly, cuts that are not as dry as shoulder cuts.

WINE SUGGESTIONS

Once you've enjoyed a dry and zesty wine as an aperitif, stick with the same wine to accompany the pâté. Choose a Muscadet de Sèvre et Maine (Loire Valley), Entre-Deux-Mers (Bordelais) or Bourgogne Aligoté.

CHEF'S TIP

*Instead of balsamic vinegar,
you can use wine vinegar or
a fruit-based vinegar.*

Potatoes Stuffed with Pork and Cheddar

MAKES 4 SERVINGS

4 large potatoes
3 tbsp (45 mL) vegetable oil
1 chopped onion
½ lb (250 g) lean ground pork
salt and pepper, to taste
8 slices of cheddar
1 tsp (5 mL) paprika

Sauce
1 avocado, diced
1 shallot*, chopped
1 tomato, seeded and diced
¼ cup (50 mL) olive oil
2 tbsp (25 mL) chopped fresh coriander*
1 tbsp (15 mL) balsamic vinegar
1 tbsp (15 mL) lime juice
salt and pepper, to taste

Pierce potatoes and bake with skins on, at 350°F (170°C), for approximately 45 minutes. Cut potatoes in half and remove pulp, leaving ¼ in (0.5 cm) on the skin, and put in a salad bowl. Set aside hollowed-out potatoes. Heat vegetable oil in a pan; add onions and cook for 2 to 3 minutes, then add ground pork. Season with salt and pepper and cook for 3 minutes. Add the potato pulp to the mixture and use it to fill hollowed-out potatoes. Place a slice of cheese on each potato and sprinkle with paprika. Broil in oven for 2 minutes. Mix together all sauce ingredients; season with salt and pepper. Sauce can be served cold with hot potatoes.

* See glossary

Lunchtime Ham and Vegetable Salad

MAKES 4 SERVINGS

3 tbsp (45 mL) olive oil
2 tbsp (25 mL) balsamic vinegar
1 tsp (5 mL) chopped fresh basil
4 eggs
30 green or yellow beans
12 snow peas
1 pepper, sliced
1 tomato, diced
1 cooked potato, cubed
1 lb (500 g) cooked ham, cubed
3 tbsp (45 mL) cheddar cheese, cubed or cut into strips
salt and pepper, to taste
2 tbsp (25 mL) chopped chives

In a salad bowl, mix together oil, balsamic vinegar and basil. Add salt and vinegar to water and boil eggs for 10 minutes. Shell eggs and set aside. Blanch beans and snow peas and rinse under cold water or use them uncooked. Mix together vegetables, ham and cheese; add vinaigrette. Garnish salad with halved eggs, season to taste with salt and pepper, then sprinkle with chives.

Ham

CHEF'S TIP

Let your imagination run wild. Replace the vegetables suggested in this recipe with other vegetables and serve them raw, if you like!

CHEF'S TIP

Just as you would with lamb, pierce the pork roast and add slivers of garlic for a tasty dish.

Cold Roast Pork, Radicchio and Mango Salad

MAKES 4 SERVINGS

VINAIGRETTE
2 tbsp (25 mL) hot mustard
2 tbsp (25 mL) orange juice
1 shallot*, chopped
3 tbsp (45 mL) olive oil
2 tbsp (25 mL) balsamic vinegar
1 tbsp (15 mL) chopped chives
salt and pepper, to taste

slices of cold roast pork, loin or leg tip roast
(see recipes on pages 169, 215 and 224)
1 radicchio, shredded
1 mango, diced or cut into julienne strips
1 tomato, sliced

Mix together mustard, orange juice and shallot, then slowly blend in olive oil. Add balsamic vinegar and chives and season with salt and pepper.

   Cut leftover roast into thin slices. Clean radicchio. Mix together radicchio, mango and vinaigrette. Add pork and tomato slices. Mix well and serve.

   Red leaf lettuce can be substituted for radicchio.

   * See glossary

Spaghetti with Pork Meat Sauce

MAKES 6 SERVINGS

3 tbsp (45 mL) olive oil
1 onion, finely minced
2 lb (1 kg) lean ground pork
4 slices of sun-dried tomatoes, chopped
1 can of tomatoes, 28 oz (796 mL)
4 cloves garlic, finely minced
1 tbsp (15 mL) dried basil
1 tsp (5 mL) pili-pili* pepper, chopped
1 package of spaghetti noodles, 1 lb (500 g)
salt and pepper, to taste
2 tbsp (25 mL) chopped fresh parsley
butter or cream in sufficient quantity to reheat pasta

Heat olive oil in a pan and cook onion and ground pork for 5 to 6 minutes, over medium heat. Add sun-dried tomatoes, canned tomatoes, minced garlic, basil and pili-pili. Mix and cook over low heat, covered, for 30 minutes.

In a large pot, boil water, adding a few drops of olive oil. Cook spaghetti noodles for 5 to 6 minutes. Drain and set aside. Season sauce with salt and pepper, then add chopped parsley. Reheat pasta with butter or cream for 1 to 2 minutes; cover with sauce and serve immediately.

* See glossary

Ground pork

CHEF'S TIP

You can also make this dish with lasagna or cannelloni.

WINE SUGGESTIONS

Think Italian and choose simple and supple wines with plenty of color and substance. Sangiovese de Romagna and Rosso di Montalcino (Tuscany), served at between 60 and 64°F (16 and 18°C), are excellent selections.

CHEF'S TIP

Avoid heating olive oil excessively; vegetable oil works equally well.

WINE SUGGESTIONS

Any dry or medium-dry supple white wines with a fairly pronounced bouquet — Alsace wines, or wines from the Loire Valley, Anjou and Vouvray (dry or medium-dry) — are the perfect foil for the flavors and aromas of the curry and other condiments used in this recipe. Viognier (Languedoc) is another excellent accompaniment.

* slices of boneless sirloin tip, slices of loin roast or loin chops

Curry Coconut Steaks

MAKES 4 SERVINGS

3 tbsp (45 mL) olive oil
4 pork steaks, cut from loin or leg,
about 1 in (2 cm) thick
salt and pepper, to taste
1 onion, sliced
1 clove garlic, minced
1 green pepper, cubed
½ red pepper, cut into julienne strips
2 celery stalks, diced
1 cup (250 mL) chicken broth
2 tbsp (25 mL) curry powder
2 zucchini, cut into pieces, or baby squash, quartered
¼ cup (50 mL) coconut milk or whipping cream (35%)

Heat oil in pan, season steaks with salt and pepper and cook for 2 to 3 minutes; remove steaks and set aside. In the same pan, sauté onion, garlic, green and red pepper and celery. Add chicken stock, then curry. Cook 3 to 4 minutes over low heat. Add steaks and mix. Add zucchini or baby squash. Cook for 3 more minutes and set aside. Add coconut milk or cream, season with salt and pepper. Serve with vegetables.

If using cream, simmer the sauce very slowly. Be careful not to overcook the zucchini or baby squash. If using coconut milk, do not let it boil.

Pork and Mozzarella Pizza

MAKES 4 SERVINGS

½ lb (250 g) bread or pizza dough, uncooked
1 pork tenderloin, 12 oz (375 g)
2 tbsp (25 mL) olive oil
salt and pepper, to taste
2 tbsp (25 mL) mild mustard
3 tbsp (45 mL) spicy Diana sauce*
1 tsp (5 mL) oregano
2 courgettes (zucchinis), thinly sliced
2 tbsp (25 mL) olive oil**
5 mL (1 tsp) Herbes de Provence*
½ lb (250 g) red or yellow cherry tomatoes
10 slices of mozzarella

Spread the dough into a circle with a 10 to 12 in (25 to 30 cm) circumference. Place dough on a pizza pan or baking sheet. Cut the tenderloin into fairly thin slices. Heat 2 tbsp (25 mL) of oil in a nonstick pan. Season tenderloin slices with salt and pepper and brown for 1 to 2 minutes on each side. Remove from heat and let cool. Mix together mustard, Diana sauce and oregano. Spread the mixture over the dough and add tenderloin slices. Mix zucchini with 2 tbsp (25 mL) of oil and Herbes de Provence and marinate for 10 minutes. Place marinated zucchini on dough and add tomato slices. Top with mozzarella cheese. Bake in oven at 325°F (160°C) for 15 to 20 minutes. Serve piping hot.

See glossary
** *Olive oil is used twice in this recipe*

Tenderloin

CHEF'S TIP

If you can't find Diana sauce, use chili sauce.

WINE SUGGESTIONS

Here, spicy Diana sauce combines with the other ingredients to make a pizza that's an excellent companion for vigorous and fairly full-bodied Italian reds. From Umbria, Torgiano Rosso, with its rich color and intriguing bouquet, is sure to enchant even the most discriminating of oenophiles.

Ground pork

CHEF'S TIP

Ground pork, like all ground meats should be cooked until no longer pink, 170°F (80°C)

WINE SUGGESTIONS

Energetic, light and unpretentious white wines, such as Vinho Verde (Portugal) or Picpoul de Pinet (Coteaux du Languedoc) are the perfect match for these brochettes and their colorful onions. Serve well chilled (46°F / 8°C).

Pork Medallions and Ground Pork with Roasted Onions

MAKES 4 SERVINGS

½ lb (250 g) lean ground pork
1 tbsp (15 mL) soy sauce
2 tbsp (25 mL) chopped fresh parsley
salt and pepper, to taste
4 pork tenderloin medallions, about 3½ oz (100 g) each
2 tbsp (25 mL) vegetable oil
2 onions, minced
45 mL (3 tbsp) balsamic vinegar

Mix together ground pork, soy sauce and chopped parsley. Season lightly with salt and pepper. Shape into patties, about 3½ oz (100 g) each. Alternate tournedos and patties on skewers. In a small amount of oil, grill or fry brochettes for 4 to 5 minutes, then continue cooking in oven at 325°F (160°C) for 5 minutes. Cook onions in same cooking oil for 4 minutes, until transparent. Add balsamic vinegar. Turn heat off and cover pan. Remove brochettes from oven, arrange around edge of serving dish with onions in the center of dish.

Decorate with small sprigs of parsley.

Recipes for Two
Bon appétit!

WINE SUGGESTIONS

Rosé wines served well chilled will add a touch of elegance to this meal and counter the strong flavors of the marinade. Choose wines from Italy, Spain or the South of France, dry, with a slight bite.

Spicy Pork Kabobs with Puff Pastry

MAKES 2 SERVINGS

1 tbsp (15 mL) tamari* sauce
1 tbsp (15 mL) honey
1 tbsp (15 mL) chili sauce
¼ tsp (1 mL) garlic powder
¼ tsp (1 mL) ground ginger
½ lb (250 g) pork cubes, split and flattened
2 tbsp (25 mL) vegetable oil
½ package ½ lb (250 g) ready-to-use puff pastry
1 egg yolk
2 tbsp (25 mL) milk
salt and pepper, to taste
¼ tsp (1 mL) dried crushed chilies

Prepare a marinade with the tamari sauce, honey, chili sauce, garlic and ginger and mix thoroughly. Marinate cubes for 15 to 20 minutes, stirring often. Heat vegetable oil and brown pork cubes over high heat for 2 minutes. Remove cubes from pan, drain and let cool.

Roll puff pastry into 2 strips, 6 x 4 in (15 x 10 cm) each. Mix together the egg yolk and milk. Brush pastry strips with mixture. Cook in oven for 5 minutes at 400°F (200°C). Remove from oven and let cool. Thread brochette cubes on skewers; brush with marinade mixture. Season with salt and pepper. Place pork on precooked pastry strips and cook in 350°F (180°C) oven for 7 to 8 minutes. Brush with marinade during cooking. Sprinkle with crushed chilies. Serve when very hot and crisp.

* See glossary

Marinated Shrimp and Pork Kabobs

MAKES 2 SERVINGS

8 large shrimp (21 to 25 per pound)
8 pork cubes, ¾ in (2 cm)
3 tbsp (45 mL) oyster sauce
2 tbsp (25 mL) lime juice
3 tbsp (45 mL) olive oil
2 tbsp (25 mL) shallots*
⅓ cup (75 mL) dry white wine
¼ cup (50 mL) whipping cream (35%)
1 tomato, diced
1 green onion
salt and pepper, to taste

Marinate shrimp and pork cubes in oyster sauce, lime juice and olive oil for 15 minutes. Stir often. In a saucepan, combine shallots and dry white wine and reduce to three-quarters of original quantity. Add cream, tomato and onion. Reduce again for about 2 minutes and season with salt and pepper.

Alternate pork and shrimp on wooden skewers and broil gently on preheated grill or on baking sheet for 4 minutes. Place in 325°F (160°C) oven, cover and cook for 2 to 3 minutes longer.

Remove kabobs from oven, place on individual plates or a serving dish and cover with sauce. Can be served with plain white rice, vegetable rice or wild rice.

* See glossary

Cubes for kabobs

CHEF'S TIP

For this recipe, use only large shrimp; smaller shrimp will cook faster than the pork and will dry out.

WINE SUGGESTIONS

Because of the cream sauce, dry but supple white wines are best with these shrimp and pork cube brochettes for two. California Chardonnay wines, Mâcon-Villages and Saint-Véran (Burgundy) or a suave Soave of good vintage (Veneto) should be served at 50°F (10°C).

Loin, center-cut

or chops

CHEF'S TIP

Smaller, standard scallops are a good substitute for the larger "coquille Saint-Jacques" variety.

WINE SUGGESTIONS

A supple Chardonnay is a good match for the special texture of scallops and the smooth cream-and-vermouth sauce. Choose from Saint-Véran, Montagny or Pouilly-Fuissé (Burgundy). Serve chilled, but not excessively so (50 to 54°F/ 10 to 12°C)

Chops with Scallops

MAKES 2 SERVINGS

2 pork chops, 1½ in (4 cm) thick
salt and pepper, to taste
2 tbsp (25 mL) vegetable oil
6 sea scallops, fresh or frozen
1 tbsp (15 mL) butter
1 shallot*, chopped
¼ cup (50 mL) French vermouth
3 tbsp (45 mL) whipping cream (35%)
¼ cup (50 mL) chicken broth
1 tbsp (15 mL) fresh parsley, chopped

Season both sides of chops with salt and pepper and brown gently in hot oil for 3 minutes. Place chops on a baking sheet and bake at 325°F (160°C) for 4 to 5 minutes. Brown scallops in same cooking oil for 2 minutes, remove from pan and set aside. Melt butter in a clean pan and cook dried shallot until transparent, about 2 minutes. Add vermouth, cream and broth. Let mixture simmer until reduced by half. Place chops on individual plates, add three scallops to each plate, then spoon on sauce, seasoning with salt, pepper and a sprinkle of parsley.

If the sauce is too thin, thicken with a mixture of equal quantities of very cold butter and flour or add 1 tbsp (15 mL) cornstarch, mixed into 2 tbsp (25 mL) of cold water.

* See glossary

Crisp Herbed Spareribs

MAKES 2 SERVINGS

1½ lb (750 g) back ribs
1 onion
2 cloves
1 bay leaf
1 sprig of thyme
salt, to taste
2 tbsp (25 mL) mild mustard
1 tbsp (15 mL) tamari* sauce
1 tbsp (15 mL) ketchup
1 tbsp (15 mL) chopped fresh parsley
1 tbsp (15 mL) chopped fresh coriander*
or ¼ tsp (1 mL) ground coriander
⅓ cup (75 mL) bread crumbs
salt and pepper, to taste

Separate spareribs into individual ribs. Place spareribs in 10 cups (2.5 L) water, with onion, cloves, bay leaf and thyme. Season moderately with salt. Cook for 45 minutes, over medium heat. Drain and set aside. In a bowl, mix together mustard and tamari sauce. Add ketchup, parsley and coriander. Mix thoroughly. Brush spareribs with mixture, sprinkle with bread crumbs and cook on grill or in oven. Season with additional salt and pepper to taste. Broil in oven for 4 to 5 minutes, or barbecue for 2 to 3 minutes.

See glossary

Back ribs or spareribs

(fresh)

CHEF'S TIP

The marinade can be prepared ahead of time and stored in a jar. Instead of marinating spareribs for 15 to 20 minutes, brush them with the mixture at the last minute.

WINE SUGGESTIONS

For grilled spareribs, your best choices are fruity and young reds produced with Gamay grapes; for example, the flavorful wines of the Beaujolais region. Beaujolais-Village, Chiroubles or their neighbor and cousin Coteaux du Lyonnais, served slightly chilled, are all excellent alternatives.

Cutlets

CHEF'S TIP

This recipe can also be prepared with ready-to-use guacamole (purée of avocado).

WINE SUGGESTIONS

Smoothness and strength of character are the main characteristics of this particular recipe, which is delicious with a dry but fairly energetic white wine with noticeable refinement. Hermitage Blanc (Rhône) for those who can afford it, a relatively aged Savennières (Anjou) or an excellent Château de Pessac-Léognan (Bordeaux, Graves) are good choices. Serve at about 50°F (10 °C).

Pork Cutlets with Avocado and Spinach

MAKES 2 SERVINGS

4 boneless pork cutlets, about ½ in (1 cm) thick
4 spinach leaves
2 slices Jura Flore, Gruyère or Swiss cheese
½ avocado, sliced
salt and freshly ground pepper, to taste
1 tbsp (15 mL) olive oil
½ red pepper, diced
¼ cup (50 mL) brown veal stock*
2 tbsp (25 mL) whipping cream (35%)
1 tbsp (15 mL) hot mustard

Flatten cutlets between two sheets of plastic wrap. Cover two cutlets with spinach leaves, cheese and avocado. Season with salt and pepper. Cover each cutlet with a second cutlet and press together firmly. For sauce, heat olive oil and sauté pepper over high heat for 2 to 3 minutes, add veal stock, cream and mustard, then season with salt and pepper. In a very small amount of fat, cook cutlets in a nonstick pan for 2 to 3 minutes. Place cutlets on a foil-lined baking sheet and cook in oven for 3 minutes at 325°F (160°C). Pour sauce to cover bottom of each plate, add cutlets, then cover them with remaining sauce. Sprinkle with freshly ground pepper and serve immediately.

* You may substitute beef broth or bouillon

Pepper-Stuffed Cutlets

MAKES 2 SERVINGS

2 tbsp (25 mL) olive oil
1 green pepper, minced
salt and pepper, to taste
1 tbsp (15 mL) brown sugar
1 tbsp (15 mL) grated ginger
5 oz (150 g) lean ground pork
2 pork cutlets, flattened
small amount of olive oil to brush cutlets
2 tbsp (25 mL) butter
1 shallot*, chopped
¼ cup (50 mL) chopped mushrooms
4 small zucchinis
½ red pepper, seeded and sliced in julienne strips
¼ cup (50 mL) whipping cream (35%)
¼ cup (50 mL) cider

In a pan, heat olive oil and cook green peppers for 4 to 5 minutes over medium heat. Season with salt and pepper. Add brown sugar, ginger and ground pork and cook for 1 to 2 minutes. Remove from heat and place in a bowl. Place a small amount of stuffing in center of cutlets, roll into a cigar shape and place in an ovenproof dish after brushing lightly with oil. Cook in oven for 5 to 7 minutes at 350°F (180°C). Lower temperature to 300°F (150°C) and cook for 5 more minutes, covered.

Melt butter in a pan, add shallot and mushrooms and cook for 2 to 3 minutes. Add miniature zucchinis and red pepper, cooking for 1 to 2 minutes. Add cream and cider and cook sauce for 3 to 4 minutes. Season with salt and pepper. Cover bottom of serving dish with sauce, peppers and zucchinis. Arrange stuffed cutlets on top.

* See glossary

CHEF'S TIP

Never confuse sweet and hot peppers — the difference is crucial!

WINE SUGGESTIONS

Cabernet wines are reminiscent of the appealing aroma typical of peppers. Choose from among very supple red wines for this smooth and flavorful dish. Anjou Village or Bourgueil wines (Loire Valley) and Bordeaux wines, slightly aged (about 5 years) are sure to please the palate.

Tenderloin

Chef's Tip

In Europe, pork tenderloin is known as filet mignon. It is available fresh or frozen.

Wine Suggestions

Sweet and smooth-tasting peaches and hot mustard are combined with a citrus sauce in a dish best set off by a fruity white wine with a strong personality. Oenophiles with a penchant for Alsace wines will undoubtedly choose a vintage Riesling, and those who swear only by Gewürztraminer wines will find in them a more than ample source of inspiration.

Tenderloin Stuffed with Peaches

MAKES 2 SERVINGS

1 pork tenderloin, 12 oz (375 g)
¼ lb (125 g) lean ground pork
2 fresh or canned peaches
salt and pepper, to taste
1 tbsp (15 mL) hot mustard
2 tbsp (25 mL) bread crumbs

Sauce
2 tbsp (25 mL) butter
1 small onion, minced
2 fresh or canned peaches
1 clove garlic, minced
¼ cup (50 mL) orange juice
salt and pepper, to taste
3 tbsp (45 mL) brown veal stock*
1 tbsp (15 mL) chopped fresh parsley

Split the tenderloin down the center. Mix together ground pork and first two peaches, cut into pieces. Season with salt and pepper. Fill inside of tenderloin with stuffing; tie with butcher's twine and place seam side down. Brush tenderloin with mustard and roll in bread crumbs. Season with salt and pepper. Place on slightly oiled baking sheet. Cook for 15 minutes in 325°F (160°C) oven. Lower temperature to 250°F (120°C) and cook for 20 minutes.

Sauce
Melt butter in saucepan, add onion and 2 remaining peaches; cook for 3 to 4 minutes. Add garlic and orange juice, season with salt and pepper and cook for about 2 minutes. Add veal stock and chopped parsley. Cut tenderloin into 1 in (2 cm) slices and serve in a pool of sauce.

* You may substitute with beef broth or bouillon

Tenderloin Stuffed with Greens and Chives

MAKES 2 SERVINGS

1 whole 12 oz (375 g) pork tenderloin
¼ lb (125 g) lean ground pork
1 shallot, chopped*
1 tbsp (15 mL) chopped nuts
2 tbsp (25 mL) tarragon mustard
1 tbsp (15 mL) Worcestershire sauce
1 egg
salt and pepper, to taste
8 Iceberg lettuce
or green cabbage leaves
1 pig's stomach lining
1 tsp (5 mL) Herbes de Provence*

Sauce
2 tbsp (25 mL) unsalted butter
1 shallot*, chopped
2 tbsp (25 mL) chopped chives
¼ cup (50 mL) whipping cream (35%)
3 tbsp (45 mL) Pineau des Charentes**
salt and pepper, to taste

WINE SUGGESTIONS

Although very refined, this dish is still quite flavorful and very smooth. The challenge here is to choose aromatic and supple white wines that are rich enough to make a good match: Chardonnay du Penedés (Spain) and, for lovers of Rhône Valley wines, a Crozes-Hermitage or a rare Châteauneuf-du-Pape.

Split the tenderloin and shape into a square or rectangle. Mix together ground pork, shallot, nuts, mustard, Worcestershire sauce and egg. Season with salt and pepper. Blanch lettuce or cabbage leaves in boiling salted water for about 1 minute. Cool in cold water. Roll stuffing into a sausage shape and wrap with half the lettuce leaves. Season the tenderloin with salt and pepper and place the stuffing in its center. Close and roll. Wrap the tenderloin with lettuce leaves and stomach lining. Add Herbes de Provence. Cook tenderloin on a baking sheet for 17 to 20 minutes in a 350°F (180°C) oven.

Melt butter in a saucepan and cook shallot for 2 to 3 minutes, until transparent. Add chives, cream and Pineau des Charentes. Let simmer for 3 minutes. Season with salt and pepper and blend in food processor. Cover bottom of serving dish with sauce. Cut tenderloin into slices and serve.

* See glossary
** If necessary, you may substitute Italian vermouth

*Loin steaks**

CHEF'S TIP

For this recipe you can also use canned or dried tomatoes.

WINE SUGGESTIONS

The texture produced by this particular cooking method and the condiments it involves call for vigorous, aromatic and supple red wines. Try a Merlot from Italy (Grave del Friuli) or Chile for friendly get-togethers, or a robust and sensual red Côte de Provence for dining à deux.

* or tenderloin medallions

Small Medallions with Sesame Seeds

MAKES 2 SERVINGS

2 tomatoes
4 boneless center cut pork chops about 3½ oz (100 g) each,
¾ inch (1.75 cm) thick
1 tbsp (15 mL) hot mustard
1 tbsp (15 mL) sesame seeds
2 tbsp (25 mL) olive oil
1 shallot*, chopped
1 tsp (5 mL) chopped garlic
1 tsp (5 mL) shredded fresh basil leaves**
½ cup (125 mL) beef or chicken broth
salt and pepper, to taste
pinch of sugar (optional)

Blanch tomatoes in boiling water, trim and chop coarsely. Brush medallions with mustard and sprinkle with sesame seeds. In a skillet, heat olive oil and brown medallions for 2 to 3 minutes on each side. Roast medallions in ovenproof dish and bake at 325°F (160°C) for 3 minutes. Add shallot to the skillet; mix in tomatoes, chopped garlic and basil leaves. Cook for 10 minutes over medium heat. Add stock and blend in food processor until barely mixed. Return to heat, season with salt and pepper and add a pinch of sugar, if desired. Cover the bottom of individual plates with sauce and add medallions. Serve.

* See glossary
** See Fresh herbs in glossary

Oven-Baked Spareribs

MAKES 2 SERVINGS

1 slab of side ribs, about 2¼ lb (1 kg)
3 tbsp (45 mL) honey
1 clove garlic, chopped
½ tsp (2 mL) Tabasco sauce
3 tbsp (45 mL) tamari* sauce
3 tbsp (45 mL) olive oil
1 onion, minced
½ cup (125 mL) red wine
⅓ cup (75 mL) bread crumbs
salt and pepper, to taste

Cook ribs in salted water for 45 minutes, in oven or on stovetop, until tender. Prepare marinade using honey, garlic, Tabasco and tamari sauces and refrigerate for 30 minutes. Heat olive oil and cook onion for 7 minutes. Add red wine and reduce until almost all liquid has evaporated and onion is almost transparent and red wine is absorbed. Place ribs on a baking sheet, brush with marinade and sprinkle with onion and bread crumbs. Season with salt and pepper. Bake in a 350 to 375°F (180 to 190°C) oven for about 5 minutes.

* See glossary

Back ribs or spareribs

(fresh)

CHEF'S TIP

A slab of side ribs is the entire piece.

WINE SUGGESTIONS

With this dish, featuring a combination of spicy marinade and smooth honey, sensual red wines with bouquet to spare are an electrifying choice. Generous Nebbiolo d'Alba (Piedmont) wines, woody and vanilla-tinged Rioja Reserva selections and assertive Dão wines (Portugal) served at between 60 and 65°F (16 and 18°C) are excellent.

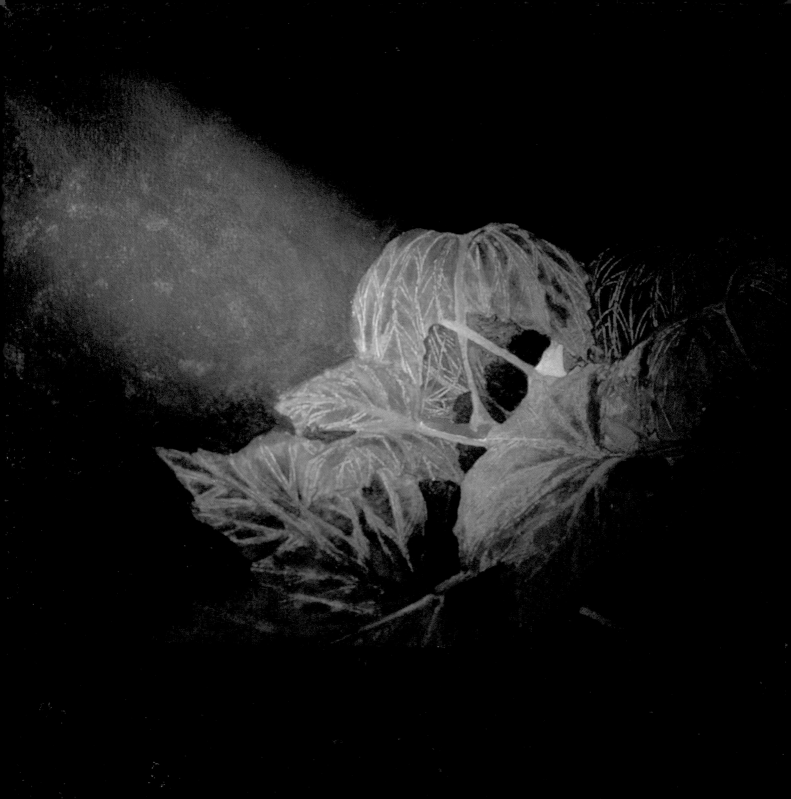

For Discriminating Gourmets

Delicious!

Cubes for kabobs

CHEF'S TIP

The term "blanquette" is usually reserved for veal, but it can also be used to refer to other types of meat.

WINE SUGGESTIONS

This ménage à trois of pork, potatoes and cream is more than enough of an incentive to choose supple but fresh white wines, such as certain Chardonnays from Chile or the South of France (Vin de Pays d'Oc, for example). Serve at 50°F (10°C).

Blanquette of Pork and Green Apples

MAKES 4 SERVINGS

2 lb (1 kg) pork cubes cut
from loin or leg
1 onion, sliced
1 carrot, peeled
1 celery stalk, minced
1 bouquet garni*
salt and pepper, to taste
4 cups (1 L) apple juice
1 cup (250 mL) cider

3 green apples
2 tbsp (25 mL) cornstarch
2 tbsp (25 mL) water
4 egg yolks
⅓ cup (75 mL) whipping
cream (35%)
4 green onions, green part only
1 tbsp (15 mL) chopped chives

In a large saucepan, cover pork cubes with water and blanch for 2 to 3 minutes. Drain. In another saucepan, combine onion, carrot, celery and bouquet garni. Season lightly with salt and pepper. Add pork cubes, apple juice and cider and cook over medium heat, for 1 hour to 1 hour and 15 minutes. When cubes are tender and sufficiently cooked, drain meat, reserving juices.

Peel and core apples. Cut apples into small oval-shaped pieces. Return cooking juices to heat, dilute cornstarch in water and add to the hot liquid. Mix together egg yolks and cream and gradually add the mixture to the sauce; cook until thickened. Remove from heat, stir for 1 to 2 minutes, then return to very low heat. Do not boil. Add apple pieces and green onion, and cook over very low heat for 3 to 4 minutes. Add pork cubes and simmer very gently. Add chives and season with salt and pepper, if necessary.

* *See glossary*

Rack of Pork with Creamy Garlic

MAKES 6 SERVINGS

1 rack of pork, from 2 to 3 lb (1 to 1.5 kg)
salt and pepper, to taste
3 tbsp (45 mL) vegetable oil
1 onion, coarsely chopped
1 carrot, coarsely chopped
1 leek, coarsely chopped
2 celery stalks
2 cups (500 mL) chicken broth
¾ cup (175 mL) garlic cloves
¾ cup (175 mL) whipping cream (35%)
2 tbsp (25 mL) butter

Ask your butcher to prepare a rack of pork. Season the rack generous-ly with salt and pepper. Heat a cast-iron Dutch oven, add oil and brown the roast on all sides, over medium heat. Add the vegetables, except gar-lic, add broth, then cook in oven for 1 hour and 15 minutes at 350°F (180°C).

Strain the cooking broth and pour into a pan; add garlic and cream. Season with salt, to taste, and cook for 15 minutes over medium heat. Blend the mixture in a food processor and add butter. Reheat the roast in aluminum foil, in a medium oven, 325 to 350°F (160 to 180°C), for 7 to 10 minutes, then slice. Serve with sauce, assorted vegetables and additional garlic, roasted whole, in oven.

Rack of pork

WINE SUGGESTIONS

*The cooking method and the use of vegetables and cream suggest a supple and dry white wine, relatively full-bodied, with enough acidity to bring out the best in this dish. Stray from the beaten path and choose a **Corbières Blanc (Languedoc)**, a **Roussette de Savoie** or the excellent and all-too-rare **Côtes du Jura**.*

CHEF'S TIP

*Well cooked or served
medium (75°F/160°C), in
my opinion this is one of the
best pork cuts.*

WINE SUGGESTIONS

*For this braised pork dish,
select a delicate, supple
gourmet wine
(to highlight the cream)
that is relatively simple.
The Bordeaux wine used
in the recipe naturally
suggests a Château wine
of the same appellation or
Premières Côtes de Blaye
vintages. Regardless of your
choice, let the wine breathe
in a carafe and serve at
about 60°F (16°C).*

Braised Rack of Pork with Pearl Onions and Apricots

MAKES 6 TO 8 SERVINGS

2 cloves garlic, slivered
3¼ lb (1.5 kg) rack of pork
3 tbsp (45 mL) vegetable oil
2 cups (500 mL) beef or chicken broth
3 tbsp (45 mL) red Bordeaux wine
½ cup (125 mL) pearl onions, peeled
2 oz (50 g) butter
2 oz (50 g) flour
¼ cup (50 mL) whipping cream (35%)
salt and pepper, to taste
8 fresh or canned apricots

Pierce roast and insert garlic slivers. In an ovenproof dish, heat vegetable oil and brown loin roast. Cook in 350°F (180°C) oven for 1 hour and 30 minutes to 1 hour and 45 minutes. Add broth, wine, pearl onions and cook for 15 minutes more. Remove from oven and cover with aluminum foil.

Strain cooking juices and reserve for onions. Melt butter in another pan and add flour to make a roux. Wet with cooking juices. Add cream, reduce to desired consistency and season with salt and pepper. On a baking sheet, caramelize apricots and pearl onions with a small amount of butter for 10 minutes in a 350°F (180°C) oven. Place the rack on a serving dish, surround with apricots and pearl onions, add sauce and serve.

Pork Loin Stuffed with Herbes de Provence

MAKES 6 TO 8 SERVINGS

3 lb (1.5 kg) boneless pork loin
3 tbsp (45 mL) hot mustard
2 tbsp (25 mL) Herbes de Provence*
¾ lb (375 g) lean ground pork
1 egg
3 tbsp (45 mL) butter
12 mushrooms, minced
1 shallot, chopped
2 tbsp (25 mL) chopped fresh parsley
2 tbsp (25 mL) chopped fresh coriander*
salt and pepper, to taste
1 cup (250 mL) beef or chicken broth

Cut a pocket in the roast, large enough for stuffing. Brush with mustard and sprinkle with Herbes de Provence. For stuffing, mix together ground pork and egg. Melt butter, and sauté mushrooms and shallot for 3 to 4 minutes. Add the mixture directly to the stuffing. Add parsley and coriander and season with salt and pepper. Stuff the loin roast. Close cavity, secure with string and cook in oven for 1 hour and 35 minutes to 1 hour and 45 minutes, at 325°F (160°C). Baste with bouillon throughout cooking. When roast is done, let rest in its cooking juices for 10 minutes. Slice to serve.

See glossary

Boneless loin roast

WINE SUGGESTIONS

The Herbes de Provence used in this recipe go best with full-bodied red wines with a sustained fragrance. Coteaux d'Aix, Les Baux (Provence), Gigondas en Côtes du Lubéron (Rhône Valley) or Côtes du Roussillon-Villages are excellent choices.

Loin, center-cut

or chops

CHEF'S TIP

Fiddleheads are so named because of their shape. They are available fresh in the springtime and frozen in other seasons.

WINE SUGGESTIONS

This recipe gets its color from tomatoes, its texture from chops and its smoothness from cream. Good reasons to choose a vigorous rosé, dry but supple, as Côtes de Provence or Côtes du Frontonnais wines usually are – rest assured they won't be playing second fiddle!

Loin Chops with Fiddleheads

MAKES 4 SERVINGS

2 cups (500 mL) fiddleheads, fresh or frozen
3 tbsp (45 mL) vegetable oil
4 pork chops, 1 in (2 cm) thick
1 onion, minced
1 tomato, peeled and chopped
1 clove garlic, chopped
salt and pepper, to taste
2 tbsp (25 mL) unsalted butter
2 tbsp (25 mL) freshly squeezed orange juice
½ cup (125 mL) whipping cream (35%)
3 tbsp (45 mL) diced yellow or green pepper (optional)

Rinse fiddleheads and steam for 3 to 4 minutes to preserve maximum flavor. Rinse in ice-cold water and set aside. In a skillet, heat oil, then brown chops on both sides for 2 minutes. Remove chops from skillet, and in same pan, cook onion and tomato, stirring constantly, for 2 to 3 minutes, then add garlic. Season with salt and pepper and set aside.

In another pan, melt butter and sauté fiddleheads for 2 minutes. Add orange juice and cream and cook mixture for 1 minute. Season with salt and pepper. Place fiddleheads in serving dish, surround with chops and coat with cooking juices. If desired, add diced yellow or green pepper.

This recipe can also be prepared with boneless pork chops, about 1 in (2 cm) thick.

Cordon Bleu Chops
with Demi-Glace Sauce

MAKES 4 SERVINGS

4 pork loin chops, 7 oz (200 g) each, 1 in (2 cm) thick, cut from the loin
salt and pepper, to taste
4 slices of Gruyère cheese
4 thin slices of ham
2 tbsp (25 mL) vegetable oil

Sauce
⅓ cup (75 mL) port
1 shallot*, minced
¾ cup (175 mL) brown veal stock**
3 tbsp (45 mL) fresh butter, cut into small pieces
salt and pepper, to taste

Cut a pocket in the center of chops to insert dressing; do not split completely. Season sparingly with salt and pepper, then insert cheese slice and ham slice and fold inward. Close and press down slightly on each chop. Cook chops in a nonstick pan, in vegetable oil, for 3 to 4 minutes on each side. Continue cooking the chops for 4 minutes in a 325°F (160°C) oven.

Sauce
Pour port into a flameproof dish, add minced shallot and reduce until almost dry. Wet with brown veal stock and let cook for 2 to 3 minutes, then remove from heat and add small pieces of butter. Season with salt and pepper, then set aside. Cover bottom of individual plates with sauce and add chops. Serve with mashed potatoes, puréed vegetables or garden-fresh vegetables.

See glossary
** *You may substitute beef broth or bouillon*

Boneless chops, for stuffing

CHEF'S TIP

The cordon bleu cutlet is a culinary classic. This recipe uses pork instead of veal.

WINE SUGGESTIONS

Fine red wines, fruity and supple, are always sure to please gourmets since they tend to enhance the texture of meats. A Côtes de Beaune-Villages (Burgundy) or a Bourgueil (Loire Valley), served at 59°F (15°C), never fails to please.

CHEF'S TIP

If you barbecue side ribs, brush them often as they cook.

WINE SUGGESTIONS

Choose full-bodied and generous red wines with a certain degree of refinement, or dry, aromatic and fruity rosés. I suggest that you look to the South of France, for a Côtes de Provence, Baux de Provence or Coteaux Varois. Any one of the three will bring back memories of European holidays!

Spareribs with Sun-Dried Tomatoes

MAKES 4 SERVINGS

12 cups (3 L) water for cooking
1 onion
1 bouquet garni*
salt and pepper, to taste
2 slabs of side ribs, 2 lb (900 g) each
2 tbsp (25 mL) tamari* sauce
1 clove garlic, minced
1 tbsp (15 mL) Worcestershire sauce
6 slices sun-dried tomatoes
2 tbsp (25 mL) honey
2 tbsp (25 mL) basil

Bring water to a boil and add onion and bouquet garni. Season with salt and pepper, then add spareribs and simmer for 45 minutes. Cut slab into individual ribs. Make a marinade with the tamari sauce, garlic, Worcestershire sauce, tomatoes, honey and basil. Season sparingly with salt and pepper. Place spareribs on a baking sheet and brush regularly with marinade during cooking. Let cook for 5 minutes in a 400°F (200°C) oven.

* See glossary

Tenderloin Medallions with Summer Fruit

MAKES 2 SERVINGS

3 tbsp (45 mL) butter
1 pork tenderloin, 12 oz (375 g) cut into 4 medallions
salt and pepper, to taste
2 dried shallots*, chopped
1 clove garlic, chopped
⅓ cup (75 mL) apple juice
½ cup (125 mL) reduced brown veal stock or beef broth
⅓ cup (75 mL) whipping cream (35%)
½ cup (125 mL) gooseberries
2 fresh green onions, sliced
chives, to taste (optional)

In a saucepan, melt butter but do not brown it, then fry tenderloins, cut into four medallions. Season with salt and pepper during cooking and cook for 2 to 3 minutes each side. Place in an ovenproof dish and continue cooking for 5 to 6 minutes in a 325°F (160°C) oven. In a pan, cook shallots for 1 to 2 minutes. Add garlic and apple juice. Reduce to three-quarters of original amount. Add reduced brown veal stock or beef broth. Add cream and gooseberries. Let cook for 2 to 3 minutes. Place medallions on individual plates and cover generously with sauce. If desired, add sautéed green onions and chives.

See glossary

Tenderloin

CHEF'S TIP

Summer offers a wonderful array of small berries: gooseberries, currants, blueberries, blackberries! Try this recipe with any one of them.

WINE SUGGESTIONS

This dish is a rainbow of color with its summer berries and a perfect complement is a Pinot Noir wine reminiscent of the delectable taste of small red fruit. The ideal selection is a red Alsace or Sancerre wine. Or why not try an American Pinot Noir? Regardless of your choice, serve the wine slightly chilled (57°F / 14°C).

Loin rib end roast, mini-crown wrapped in back ribs

CHEF'S TIP

Of all berries, cranberries are best with braised meat. They are available fresh or in chutneys and compotes.

WINE SUGGESTIONS

The smooth and fruity cranberry sauce is perfectly underscored by a tender and vigorous red wine. Gamay de Touraine (Loire Valley), Beaujolais and Mâcon (Burgundy) are fine choices and should be served chilled (54 to 57°F / 12 to 14°C).

Roasted Mini-Crown of Pork with Cranberry Sauce

MAKES 4 TO 6 SERVINGS

1 crown mini-roast, 3 lb (1.5 kg)
salt and pepper, to taste
3 tbsp (45 mL) vegetable oil
2 onions, minced
4 cups (1 L) chicken or beef broth
6 oz (170 g) fresh or frozen cranberries
¼ cup (50 mL) brown sugar
1 bunch of fresh mint

Season the sides of the mini-crown rib roast and place it in a roasting pan. Set aside. In a saucepan heat oil and cook minced onions until slightly brown, for 3 to 4 minutes. Season with salt and pepper. Spread onions around roast and add stock. Cover with aluminum foil and cook in oven at 325 to 350°F (160 to 180°C), for 1 hour and 15 minutes. Remove foil and turn oven off, letting roast rest in oven. Strain broth and heat in saucepan. Add cranberries and brown sugar. Reduce by half, over medium heat. When mixture begins to thicken (and cranberries begin to bland into sauce) add cooked onions. Place roast on serving dish. Pour cranberry and onion sauce around roast and decorate with a small bunch of fresh mint.

Fricassée of Pork Kidneys and Mushrooms

MAKES 4 SERVINGS

4 fresh pork kidneys
4 tbsp (50 mL) vegetable oil
2 tbsp (25 mL) butter
2 cups (500 mL) brown or white mushrooms
1 tomato, diced
½ clove garlic, minced
2 tbsp (25 mL) brown veal stock*
¼ cup (50 mL) port
¼ cup (50 mL) whipping cream (35%)
salt and pepper, to taste
2 tbsp (25 mL) fresh parsley, chopped (optional)

Split kidneys in two and remove white membrane (nerve). Cut into pieces one-quarter the size of a mushroom. Soak kidneys in water and a small amount of vinegar for one hour, then drain and dry them. Heat vegetable oil and sauté kidneys over high heat for 2 to 3 minutes; remove from pan and drain. Melt butter in a clean pan. Sauté quartered mushrooms. Add kidneys and tomato and cook for 2 to 3 minutes. Wet with brown veal stock and port. Add cream and continue cooking for 3 to 4 minutes. Season with salt and pepper. Sprinkle with parsley and serve very hot. This recipe can be served with fried potatoes or rice.

It is important to sauté kidneys quickly to prevent them from hardening. Drain them well to remove excess water. If kidneys begin to boil in their own juices, stop cooking them immediately, drain and start over. For tender and slightly pink kidneys, make sure to heat oil until very hot.

* You may substitute beef broth or bouillon

Kidneys

CHEF'S TIP

This traditional bistro dish is now considered a delicacy. Proper cooking is the key to success.

WINE SUGGESTIONS

Anyone who loves the delicate flavor combination of kidneys, tomatoes and cream will also appreciate fine and supple red wines as an accompaniment. Select well-structured wines such as Bordeaux vintages (regional appellation) or other Cabernet Sauvignon wines from California or Chili. Serve at about 54°F (15°C).

CHEF'S TIP

To make things easier, use a melon baller to scoop out zucchini balls.

WINE SUGGESTIONS

Oenophiles can dip into their wine cellars for a relatively mature (5 to 8 years old) aromatic red wine from Provence or Tuscany to enjoy with this delicious sauté fragrant with basil. A Bandol Mourvèdre or Sangiovese Chianti are good choices. Serve at about 64°F (18°C).

Sautéed Marinated Pork with Zucchini Balls

MAKES 4 SERVINGS

1 lb (500 g) pork loin cubes cut in ¾ in (1.75 cm)
⅓ cup (75 mL) spicy Diana sauce*
2 tbsp (25 mL) Worcestershire sauce
3 tbsp (45 mL) olive oil
1 onion, chopped
2 tomatoes, diced
1 clove garlic, minced
4 zucchini
3 tbsp (45 mL) butter
1 tbsp (15 mL) cumin seeds
1 tbsp (15 mL) chopped basil leaves
fresh parsley or basil, to taste (optional)

Marinate pork cubes in Diana sauce and Worcestershire sauce for 15 to 20 minutes, stirring occasionally. Heat olive oil and cook chopped onion, then add marinated pork cubes. Cook for 3 to 4 minutes. Add diced tomatoes and chopped garlic, then cover and cook for 5 minutes. Using a melon baller, scoop zucchini pulp into balls. Heat butter and cook zucchini balls for 3 to 4 minutes. Add cumin seeds and chopped basil leaves. Cook for 2 minutes. Add zucchini balls to pork mixture, reheat for 3 to 4 minutes over very low heat and serve immediately. Sprinkle dish with fresh parsley or additional fresh basil, to taste.

* See glossary

Ground Pork, Tomato and Gruyère Pie

MAKES 6 TO 8 SERVINGS

1 pie crust, ½ lb (250 g)
3 tbsp (45 mL) butter
1 onion, chopped
½ lb (250 g) lean ground pork
2 tomatoes, cut into julienne strips
1 tbsp (15 mL) Worcestershire sauce
2 tbsp (25 mL) chopped fresh parsley
1 tsp (5 mL) chopped fresh ginger
or ¼ tsp (1 mL) ground ginger
2 eggs
salt and pepper, to taste
6 slices of Gruyère cheese

Press dough into pie plate and prick the bottom and sides with a fork. Cover with aluminum foil, add dried uncooked beans to weight crust down and bake in a 300°F (150°C) oven for 5 minutes. Remove foil and beans when pie crust is baked. Melt butter in large pan and cook onion for 3 to 4 minutes. Add ground pork and tomatoes and cook for 4 to 5 minutes. Add Worcestershire sauce, parsley and ginger, cover and continue cooking over very low heat for 7 minutes. Let cool completely, then add eggs, season with salt and pepper and mix throughout. Add mixture to pie crust and cover with slices of Gruyère cheese. Bake in a 300 to 325°F (150 to 160°C) oven for 10 minutes.

For a smoother filling, along with the eggs add ⅓ cup (75 mL) whipping cream (35%).

Ground pork

CHEF'S TIP

I recommend a Gruyère or Jura Flore cheese or a genuine Parmesan (Parmigiano Reggiano).

WINE SUGGESTIONS

This original dish lends itself well to thirst-quenching reds, supple and fruity, such as Gamay wines. Gamay de Touraine (Loire Valley), Mâcon, Beaujolais-Villages or Chiroubles, are excellent choices for the more discriminating. Serve chilled, between 54 and 57°F (12 and 14°C).

Buffets and Receptions
Extraordinary!

Lean ground pork

CHEF'S TIP

Plantains are a type of banana and an excellent cooking ingredient. They are at their best when yellow or amber-colored. Avoid the green ones!

WINE SUGGESTIONS

For an aperitif, what better combination than these pork meatballs and a glass of sparkling wine. Blanquette de Limoux, Clairette de Die or Crémant de Bourgogne, served well chilled, are all welcome selections.

Cocktail Meatballs and Plantains

MAKES 4 SERVINGS

1 lb (500 g) ground pork
2 tbsp (25 mL) chopped fresh coriander*
½ tsp (2 mL) Tabasco sauce
3 tbsp (45 mL) Chinese oyster sauce
1 tsp (5 mL) chopped garlic
salt and pepper, to taste
2 tbsp (25 mL) butter
3 tbsp (45 mL) vegetable oil
3 tbsp (45 mL) olive oil
2 ripe plantains
2 tbsp (25 mL) sugar
pepper slices for garnish (optional)

In a bowl, mix together pork, coriander, Tabasco sauce, oyster sauce and garlic. Season with salt and pepper. Shape into large balls and brown in mixture of butter and vegetable oil for 3 to 4 minutes. Remove meatballs from pan and pour off fat. Add olive oil to pan and cook plantain slices over medium-high heat for 2 to 3 minutes. Continue cooking plantains in a 300°F (150°C) oven for 3 minutes, then add meatballs and continue cooking for 2 more minutes. Remove meatballs and plantains, then sprinkle with sugar. Place in a serving dish, add pepper slices, if desired, and serve with an aperitif.

❦ *Plantains are found in ethnic grocery stores, farmers' markets and some supermarkets.*

* See glossary

Pâté de Campagne with Prunes

MAKES 10 TO 12 SERVINGS

½ lb (250 g) pork fat
2 lb (1 kg) pork cubes
1 cup (250 mL) fresh parsley
2 onions, peeled and cut into pieces
6 cloves garlic, peeled
½ cup (125 mL) dry white wine
2 tbsp (25 mL) cognac
1 egg
½ tsp (2 mL) Quatre Épices*
salt and pepper, to taste
16 pitted prunes
bay leaves (optional)

Cut fat into cubes, then mix with pork cubes, parsley, onions, garlic, white wine and cognac. Marinate in the refrigerator, for 12 hours, then put mixture through meat grinder (do not use a food processor; meat should not be too finely ground). Add egg and Quatre Épices and season with salt and pepper. Place pitted prunes in the center of a terrine, cover with meat mixture and pat down. Add a few prunes to the top and add bay leaves, if desired. Cook in a bain-marie* in a 300 to 325°F (150 to 160°C) oven for 2 hours and 15 minutes. Let stand for 30 minutes; press down with a weight of about 1 lb (500 g) to prevent pâté from drying out.

🌶 *Another way to prevent the pâté from drying out is to cover the top with stomach lining. Order stomach lining also known as caul fat from your butcher about a week ahead of time. Before using, soak stomach lining in cold water for 30 minutes.*

* See glossary

Belly*

CHEF'S TIP

Using meat cut from the belly or jowl provides the perfect fat-lean ratio.

WINE SUGGESTIONS

Match this plummy entrée with a wine produced in French plum country (Agen), such as a red Buzet. Fans of Loire Valley wines might serve either a Saumur or an Anjou-Villages. These well-rounded wines with minimal tannin should be served at 54°F (15°C).

* or jowl

Strips

CHEF'S TIP

Rinse watercress in water and a bit of vinegar and dry thoroughly before using.

Pork Strips Salad with Avocados and Watercress

MAKES 4 SERVINGS

3 tbsp (45 mL) vegetable oil
½ lb (250 g) pork strips
3 tbsp (45 mL) olive oil
2 tbsp (25 mL) balsamic vinegar
2 avocados, not overly ripe
1 green onion, chopped
2 tbsp (25 mL) fresh coriander*, chopped
1 bunch of watercress
8 yellow cherry tomatoes
salt and pepper, to taste
chopped chives (optional)

Heat vegetable oil in a pan and brown strips for 5 minutes. Remove from oven and let cool. In a salad bowl, mix together olive oil and balsamic vinegar. Add avocados, chopped green onion, coriander and pork strips. Marinate in refrigerator for 15 to 20 minutes.

Rinse watercress using cold water and a small amount of vinegar. Arrange watercress in a serving dish. Surround with yellow cherry tomatoes. Season the salad with salt and pepper, if desired. Place pork strips and avocado in center of dish. Decorate with chopped chives.

* See glossary

Panini with Parmesan and Balsamic Vinegar

MAKES 4 SERVINGS

4 small panini buns*
3 tbsp (45 mL) olive oil
1 tbsp (15 mL) dried Italian herbs
½ red pepper, cut into julienne strips
½ green pepper, cut into julienne strips
8 thin slices of roast pork (see recipes on pages 169, 215 and 224)
8 slivers of Parmesan cheese
1 tbsp (15 mL) balsamic vinegar
salt and pepper, to taste
1 tbsp (15 mL) chopped chives

Cut panini in two lengthwise, brush with olive oil and sprinkle with herbs. Brush peppers with oil and grill peppers in oven for 5 to 6 minutes. Place roast pork slices on panini, then add peppers and Parmesan. Sprinkle with balsamic vinegar, season with salt and pepper, place on a baking sheet and cook in a 250 to 275°F (120 to 140°C) oven for 5 to 7 minutes. Sprinkle with chopped chives.

This dish can also be prepared with mozzarella-style cheese, in which case panini should be grilled for 1 to 2 minutes.

* *You may substitute Italian style hard rolls*

Boneless rib-end roast*

CHEF'S TIP

Panini are small sandwich rolls. Try them grilled with olive oil, a slice of roast pork and pesto. Delicioso!

WINE SUGGESTIONS

A simple rosé is the perfect partner for these Italian-style sandwiches. Try one from Italy, Spain or the South of France. All are dry and vigorous, with just the right amount of bite. Serve them well chilled.

* *or leg tip roast, boneless; or leg outside roast, boneless*

Leg tip roast,

*boneless**

WINE SUGGESTIONS

The cabbage, mustard and curry in this recipe, each highlighted with a citrus note, go naturally well with an aromatic wine such as an Alsace or a Gewürztraminer. Very dry and flavorful, these selections are always popular.

* or loin rib-end roast, boneless; or leg outside roast, boneless

Cold Roast with Orange-Marinated Cabbage

MAKES 4 SERVINGS

3 lb (1.5 kg) pork roast, leg tip or leg outside cut
(see recipes on pages 169, 215 and 224)
salt and pepper, to taste
¼ cup (50 mL) butter
2 tbsp (25 mL) chopped onion
1 head cabbage, shredded
1 clove garlic, minced
2 cups (500 mL) fresh orange juice*
2 cups (500 mL) chicken broth
½ cup (125 mL) rich yogurt (10% m.f.)
2 tbsp (25 mL) Dijon mustard
2 tbsp (25 mL) fresh orange juice
1 tbsp (15 mL) curry powder

Season roast with salt and pepper, then cook in oven, for 1 hour and 30 minutes to 1 hour and 45 minutes. Remove, cover with a tent of aluminum foil and let cool. Melt butter in a large saucepan, add chopped onions and cook for 2 to 3 minutes, until transparent. Add cabbage, stir well and cook mixture for 2 to 3 minutes. Add garlic, 2 cups (500 mL) orange juice and chicken broth. Cover with aluminum foil and cook in a 300 to 325°F (150 to 160°C) oven for 1 hour and 45 minutes to 2 hours. Remove foil 10 minutes before taking out cabbage, to allow liquid to evaporate. Then remove cabbage from oven and let cool for 3 to 4 hours. Mix together yogurt, mustard, 2 tbsp (25 mL) orange juice and curry and season with salt and pepper. Slice pork roast, then place in a serving dish with the orange-pickled cabbage. Add sauce or serve sauce separately.

* Orange juice is used twice in the recipe

Pork Roast and Bocconcini Sandwiches

MAKES 2 SERVINGS

¼ cup (50 mL) herb-flavored Boursin cheese
2 tbsp (25 mL) tarragon mustard
salt and pepper, to taste
4 slices of French bread
2 fresh bocconcini cheeses
2 tbsp (25 mL) olive oil
½ tsp (2 mL) Tabasco sauce
1 tbsp (15 mL) Herbes de Provence*
½ tsp (2 mL) garlic powder
4 lettuce leaves
6 slices of cooked pork roast, cut from the loin or leg
(see recipes on pages 169, 215 and 224)

Using a fork, mix together Boursin and mustard, then season with salt and pepper. Spread mixture on bread slices. Marinate bocconcini cheeses in olive oil, Tabasco sauce, Herbes de Provence and garlic powder for 15 minutes. Add lettuce leaves, bocconcini and pork slices to bread slices to make sandwiches.

See glossary

Leg tip roast,

*boneless**

CHEF'S TIP

This dish is ideal for an informal lunch or a buffet. Simply increase amounts according to the number of guests expected.

* or loin rib-end roast, boneless; or leg outside roast, boneless

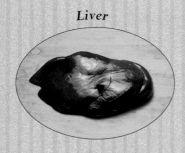

Liver

CHEF'S TIP

Some chefs use fresh side pork instead of liver, blanching it as described in this recipe.

WINE SUGGESTIONS

Choose white wines with a fruity aroma and good acidity tempered with a certain degree of suppleness. A Fiano di Avellino (Campania), a Vernaccia di San Gimignano (Tuscany) or a Cassis (white wine produced in Provence) are all worthy selections.

Liver Mousse Terrine with Almonds and Herbes de Provence

MAKES 8 TO 10 SERVINGS

2 cups (500 mL) milk
½ cup (125 mL) pork back fat
1 lb (500 g) pork liver, cleaned
3 eggs
⅓ cup (75 mL) whipping cream (35%)
2 tbsp (25 mL) cognac
½ tsp (2 mL) nutmeg
salt and pepper, to taste
2 tbsp (25 mL) slivered blanched almonds
1 tsp (5 mL) Herbes de Provence*

Heat milk and blanch small cubes of pork fat in it for 4 to 5 minutes. Remove from heat and drain. Run fat and liver through food processor until puréed. Add eggs, cream and cognac. Add nutmeg and season with salt and pepper. Place the mixture in a ceramic or cast-iron dish and sprinkle almonds and Herbes de Provence on top.

Put dish in a bain-marie* and cook in oven for 1 hour and 45 minutes to 2 hours, at 350 to 375°F (180 to 190°C). Let rest at room temperature for 3 hours, then refrigerate for at least 24 hours.

* See glossary

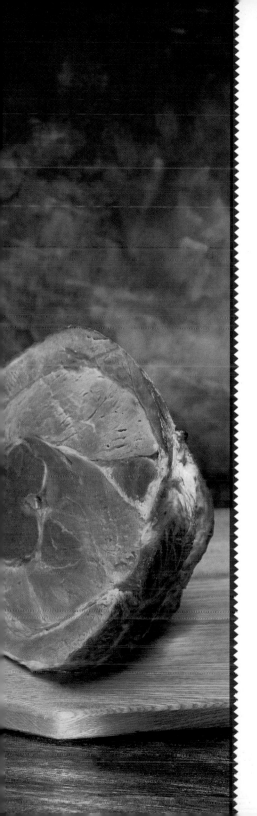

Old-Fashioned Goodness

A salute to tradition!

CHEF'S TIP

It's very important to make sure that hock is cooked thoroughly.

WINE SUGGESTIONS

Don't spend too much time worrying about a wine to go with this dish. All it needs is something simple and earthy. Serve a young Beaujolais or a Passtougrain Burgundy at 54 to 57°F (12 to 14 °C).

Pork Hocks and Vegetables

MAKES 4 SERVINGS

2 pork hocks, about 2 lb (1 kg)
1 small head cabbage
2 leeks
4 potatoes
6 baby carrots
1 head garlic, whole
1 bouquet garni*
salt, to taste

Blanch hocks in boiling water for 4 to 5 minutes, remove from water, then add washed vegetables and peeled garlic, separated into cloves. Add 16 cups (4 L) of water, covering vegetables completely. Add bouquet garni and season with salt. Cover, cook for 1 hour and 30 minutes to 2 hours. Remove vegetables from pot and continue cooking hocks for 15 to 20 minutes, uncovered. Remove skin and pull meat off the bone. Cut meat into bite-size pieces and place in a serving dish with vegetables and add a generous amount of cooking liquid. Serve with mustard, coarse salt and horseradish.

* See glossary

Pork Cubes Casserole with Beer and Celery

MAKES 4 SERVINGS

3 tbsp (45 mL) vegetable oil
1 lb (500 g) pork cubes cut from leg or loin, (¾ in, 2 cm)
1 onion, minced
4 dry apricots, halved
1 bunch celery, cut into pieces 1 to 1¼ in (2 to 3 cm) long
1 clove garlic, minced
2 bay leaves
4 cloves
1 bouquet garni*
2 cups (500 mL) beer
2 cups (500 mL) chicken broth
salt and pepper, to taste

Heat vegetable oil in a pan and cook pork cubes for 2 to 3 minutes, until browned. Place in an ovenproof dish. Add onion, apricots, celery, garlic, bay leaves, cloves and bouquet garni. Mix thoroughly. Add beer and chicken broth. Cover, place in a bain-marie* and cook in a 300°F (150°C) oven for 2 hours. Thirty minutes before cooking is completed, increase temperature to 350°F (180°C) and remove cover. Season with salt and pepper when cooking is completed, if desired. Serve as is or with baked potatoes and quartered vegetables.

* See glossary

Cubes for kabobs

CHEF'S TIP

Beer is the best match for pork cooked in this fashion. For something different, try stout.

Loin, center-cut

or chops

CHEF'S TIP

Instead of apricots, you can use figs, prunes, dates or raisins.

WINE SUGGESTIONS

The apricots and orange juice in this recipe lead me to suggest dry white Viognier wines (Condrieu and Vin de Pays selections), or a white Chenin, such as Vouvray (Touraine) or the excellent and unrecognized Savennières (Anjou).

Braised Pork Chops with Cabbage and Dried Apricots

MAKES 4 SERVINGS

3 tbsp (45 mL) butter
4 pork chops, 1½ in (4 cm) thick
3 tbsp (45 mL) vegetable oil
1 onion, chopped
1 head cabbage, cut in six wedges
12 dried apricots
2 cloves garlic, chopped
salt and pepper, to taste
½ cup (125 mL) orange juice

Melt butter in a pan and brown chops over low heat for 3 minutes on each side. Set aside. Heat oil in a Dutch oven and cook onion for 4 to 5 minutes, until transparent. Add cabbage, apricots and chops. Add chopped garlic, season with salt and pepper and add orange juice. Add 2 cups (500 mL) water, cover and cook in a 375°F (190°C) oven for 45 minutes. Reduce temperature to 300°F (150°C), remove cover and cook for 30 minutes longer. Serve in the Dutch oven, with cabbage and apricots. If desired, you can also reduce cooking juices to serve with this dish, but it is delicious as is.

Pork Mini-Sausages with Beer and Onions

MAKES 4 SERVINGS

1 lb (500 g) ground pork
3 tbsp (45 mL) spicy Diana sauce*
½ tsp (2 mL) dried tarragon
1 tbsp (15 mL) Worcestershire sauce
2 tbsp (25 mL) Provençal mustard
salt and pepper, to taste
1 pig's stomach lining**
3 tbsp (45 mL) olive oil
2 onions, sliced
3 tbsp (45 mL) wine vinegar
½ cup (125 mL) brown veal stock or thickened beef broth
1 cup (250 mL) beer
salt and pepper, to taste
1 tbsp (15 mL) chopped chives

Mix together ground pork, Diana sauce, tarragon, Worcestershire sauce and mustard. Season with salt and pepper. Shape pork into balls and wrap in stomach lining. Cook in nonstick pan for 3 to 4 minutes each side. Place in ovenproof dish and cook for 5 minutes in a 300°F (150°C) oven. In a pan, heat olive oil, add onions and cook for 4 to 5 minutes, until browned. Add wine vinegar, cook for 2 minutes, then add veal stock and beer. Cook for 3 to 4 minutes longer. Season with salt and pepper. Cover bottom of individual plates with sauce, add sausages and sprinkle with chopped chives.

See glossary
**Also known as caul fat. Before using, soak stomach lining in cold water for 30 minutes*

Ground pork and stomach lining

CHEF'S TIP

Order stomach lining from your butcher about a week before you plan to use it. If stomach lining is unavailable, wrap meat mixture in blanched cabbage leaves, spinach leaves or lettuce leaves.

Ground pork*

CHEF'S TIP

Cretons are a derivative of rillettes, which contain small chunks of meat.

WINE SUGGESTIONS

Because of their smooth texture, cretons go well with dry and medium-dry white wines, often produced with a Chenin Blanc base, of the Anjou and Touraine type. Other Anjou or Vouvray wines are equally good choices. For something less expensive and less refined, but in the same vein, why not try a South African Steen?

* or jowl or fresh side pork, put through a meat grinder

Old-Fashioned Cretons with Chives

MAKES 4 SERVINGS

3 tbsp (45 mL) lard
1 onion, finely chopped
1 shallot*, minced
2 lb (1 kg) ground pork
½ tsp (2 mL) ground nutmeg
¼ tsp (1 mL) ground cloves
½ tsp (2 mL) ground coriander
2 cloves garlic, minced
¼ cup (50 mL) gin
2 tbsp (25 mL) chopped chives
salt and pepper, to taste

In a large pot, melt lard, then brown onion and shallot for 3 minutes. Add ground pork, mix thoroughly and cook for 3 to 4 minutes over medium heat. Add nutmeg, cloves, coriander and minced garlic. Stir well and cook for 3 minutes longer. Cover and cook for 45 minutes, over very low heat. Drain and reserve cooking fat. Use a fork to blend mixture. Add the gin and one-third of the cooking fat, refrigerating remaining fat. After 30 minutes add refrigerated fat and chives. Season with salt and pepper. Place mixture in a terrine dish and refrigerate.

Cretons can be frozen, and they will keep for several weeks.

* See glossary

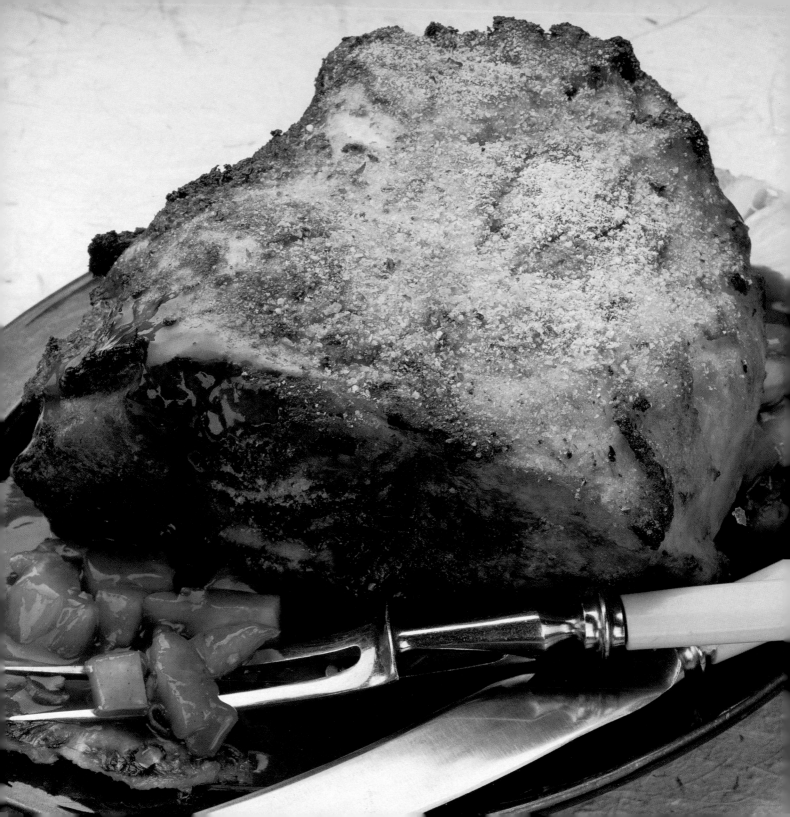

Shoulder Roast with Pumpkin and Pineapple Sauce

MAKES 4 SERVINGS

1 shoulder roast picnic or butt, 3 lb (1.5 kg), bone in
¼ cup (50 mL) mustard
2 tbsp (25 mL) pesto
salt and pepper, to taste
¼ cup (50 mL) bread crumbs
1 small pumpkin, cubed
2 cups (500 mL) orange juice
1 tbsp (15 mL) ground ginger
2 tbsp (25 mL) brown sugar
½ cup (125 mL) veal stock or thickened beef broth
4 slices fresh pineapple

Spread roast with mustard and pesto, season with salt and pepper and sprinkle with bread crumbs. Place roast in an ovenproof dish; surround with pumpkin cubes. Add orange juice and ginger and cook, covered, in a 350°F (180°C) oven for 1 hour to 1 hour and 30 minutes. Remove cover and continue cooking at 375°F (190°C) for 3 to 4 minutes, until roast begins to brown. Remove from oven and keep warm, in a cloth or aluminum foil tent. Reduce cooking juices and add brown sugar. Add veal or beef stock and cook for 2 to 3 minutes. Brown pineapple slices in a nonstick pan, for 2 to 3 minutes each side. The pineapple's natural sugar should be sufficient for browning; if not, add a small amount of fat to the pan. Remove pineapple slices, place in serving dish, cover with sauce and add roast.

CHEF'S TIP

The shoulder is a very flavorful cut. Cook roasts with the bone in.

WINE SUGGESTIONS

Pumpkin and pineapple are a wonderful combination, excellent with the slightly exotic aroma of a supple dry white wine. Chardonnay and Australian Sauvignon are good choices, served chilled at between 46 and 50°F (8 and 10°C).

CHEF'S TIP

This recipe makes 8 to 10 small crêpes. Make crêpes the same size as you would pancakes, and large enough to accommodate the filling.

WINE SUGGESTIONS

Because of the unique flavor and high acidity of spinach, it isn't easy to choose a wine to accompany a dish that is made with it. The crêpes, cheese and other ingredients used in this recipe are a combination sure to be delicious with a simple white wine with a Sauvignon base. Serve your selection at between 46 and 50°F (8 and 10°C).

Buckwheat Crêpes with Ground Pork and Spinach Filling

MAKES 4 TO 6 SERVINGS

Buckwheat Crêpes
½ cup (125 mL) buckwheat flour
1 egg
½ tsp (2 mL) salt
⅓ cup (75 mL) milk or water
2 tbsp (15 mL) olive oil

3 tbsp (45 mL) vegetable oil
2 shallots*, chopped
¾ lb (375 g) ground pork
salt and pepper, to taste

2 tbsp (25 mL) tomato paste
1 egg
2 tbsp (25 mL) butter
5 oz (150 g) spinach
½ tsp (2 mL) nutmeg
¼ clove garlic, chopped
8 crêpes
2 cups (500 mL) béchamel sauce*
8 slices cheddar, Gruyère
or Parmesan cheese

Make a well in the flour; mix in egg and salt. Gradually add milk or water, then olive oil. Refrigerate batter for 20 minutes before cooking the crêpes in a nonstick pan.

In a pan, heat vegetable oil and cook shallots for 2 to 3 minutes. Add ground pork and cook for 2 to 3 minutes. Season with salt and pepper. Remove from heat and add tomato paste. Mix in egg and set aside. Melt butter and cook spinach, nutmeg and garlic. Mix spinach into pork. Spread crêpes flat and add filling, then fold sides inward and place in ovenproof dish, seam side down. Add béchamel sauce; place cheese on top of crêpes. Broil for 2 to 3 minutes and serve very hot.

* See glossary

Pickled Pork Cubes

MAKES 4 SERVINGS

1 lb (500 g) fresh side pork, cubed
½ tsp (2 mL) grated nutmeg
½ tsp (2 mL) ground cinnamon
½ tsp (2 mL) dried thyme
salt and pepper, to taste
1 cup (250 mL) lard
4 shallots*, whole
1 clove garlic, whole
½ cup (125 mL) dry white wine

Mix together pork cubes, nutmeg, cinnamon and thyme. Season with salt and pepper. Refrigerate for 30 minutes. In a large saucepan, heat lard, then add pork cubes and brown for 4 to 5 minutes over medium heat. Lower heat by half and add shallots and garlic. Add white wine. Cover and cook over very low heat for 45 minutes to 1 hour. Stir often. Uncover, cook for 20 minutes longer over very low heat. Remove from heat, cover and let rest for 2 hours. Return to heat and cook for 15 to 20 minutes, covered. Remove from heat, cover and let rest again for 15 to 20 minutes. Thread cubes on skewers. Serve with a salad or with chives.

* See glossary

Belly

CHEF'S TIP

This recipe uses cubed pork cut from the belly and then pickled.

WINE SUGGESTIONS

Fleshy whites are a good match for this dish, along with delicious farmhouse bread. Look to the Rhône Valley for a simple Crozes-Hermitage or venture to an adjacent region and choose a Saint-Joseph white. Serve at 50°F (10°C).

CHEF'S TIP

This dish can be served cold, for a buffet; remember to cut slices very thin. Diced or sliced mushrooms can also be added to the Madeira sauce.

WINE SUGGESTIONS

The peppery and lightly smoky aroma of a Syrah will go marvelously well with this delicious pork dish. Languedoc wines (with a Syrah base), a moderately priced Shiraz from Australia or a Crozes-Hermitage (Rhône Valley) are good choices. Serve these wines at about 60°F (16°C).

Smoked Ham En Croûte

MAKES 6 TO 8 SERVINGS

3 lb (1.5 kg) smoked ham, boneless, fully cooked
1 package puff pastry, 1 lb (500 g)
1 egg yolk
2 tbsp (25 mL) water
3 tbsp (45 mL) Dijon mustard
2 tbsp (25 mL) chopped fresh tarragon, or 1 tbsp (15 mL) dried tarragon

Madeira Sauce
3 tbsp (45 mL) unsalted butter
½ cup (125 mL) shallot*, chopped
½ cup (125 mL) Madeira or port wine
1 cup (250 mL) brown veal stock**
¼ cup (50 mL) whipping cream (35%)
salt and pepper, to taste

Use a rolling pin to roll puff pastry into a sheet about ¾ in (1.5 cm) thick. Place ham in center of sheet; brush surrounding pastry with the egg yolk, beaten with the water. Spread the top of the ham with mustard and tarragon. Wrap the ham in the pastry, covering it completely. Turn seam side down, brush with egg yolk mixture and apply pastry cutouts for decoration. Place ham in an ovenproof dish. Cook in a 350°F (180°C) oven for 25 to 30 minutes.

In the meantime, prepare Madeira sauce as follows: melt butter in a saucepan. Add chopped shallots and cook gently for 4 to 5 minutes. Add Madeira (or port) and cook for 2 to 3 minutes longer. Add brown veal stock. Add cream and bring to a boil; season with salt and pepper. Remove ham from oven, slice and add Madeira sauce. Ham can be served with new potatoes, rice, noodles or fresh pasta.

* See glossary
** You may substitute beef broth or bouillon

Country Style Omelette

MAKES 4 SERVINGS

3 bacon strips or pancetta slices, diced
3 tbsp (45 mL) butter
¼ cup (50 mL) onion, finely chopped
5 oz (150 g) lean ground pork
1 potato, precooked, diced
2 tbsp (25 mL) chopped fresh parsley
salt and pepper, to taste
1 tbsp (15 mL) vegetable oil
10 medium-size eggs
grated Parmesan, to taste (optional)

Blanch bacon or pancetta in boiling water for 3 minutes, then drain and set aside. Melt butter in a pan, add onion and cook for 3 to 4 minutes. Add ground pork, stir and cook for 4 to 5 minutes. Add potato and chopped parsley and season with salt and pepper. Cook for 2 to 3 minutes and set aside. Heat vegetable oil in a nonstick pan. Beat eggs and add to pan. When omelette is almost set, add filling and gently flip one side inward to make a sandwich, with filling in center. Place omelette on serving dish. This dish can be served with Parmesan cheese, if desired.

This omelette is good cold, seasoned with balsamic vinegar and served with a salad.

Ground pork

CHEF'S TIP

You can also use ham or cooked pork strips to make this dish.

Ground pork

CHEF'S TIP

This culinary classic is also known as cottage pie in Britain.

WINE SUGGESTIONS

To go with this old-fashioned, practical and popular dish, choose supple, light red wines with very little tannin. Try a Gamay de Touraine, or a Beaujolais or a Merlot from Bulgaria or Italy. Be sure to serve your selection fairly well chilled (54 to 57°F / 12 to 14°C).

Pork Shepherd's Pie

MAKES 8 TO 10 SERVINGS

6 potatoes
3 tbsp (45 mL) whipping cream (35%)
1 egg yolk
3 tbsp (45 mL) butter
3 tbsp (45 mL) vegetable oil
2 onions, chopped
1 lb (500 g) lean ground pork
1 clove garlic, chopped
½ tsp (2 mL) oregano
½ tsp (2 mL) chopped fresh thyme
salt and pepper, to taste
1 can corn kernels, 12 oz (341 mL)
1 can cream corn, 14 oz (398 mL)
6 slices of mozzarella

Peel potatoes, cube and cook in salted boiling water for 20 minutes. Mash potatoes and mix in cream, egg yolk and butter. Set aside. In a pan, heat vegetable oil and cook onions, then add ground pork and cook for 4 to 5 minutes. Add garlic, oregano and thyme. Season with salt and pepper. Set aside.

Mix together drained corn kernels with cream corn. In large oven-proof dish, layer potatoes, corn and ground pork alternately, beginning and ending with potatoes. Top with mozzarella slices. Cook in a 300°F (150°C) oven for 25 to 30 minutes.

Sausage Patties with Pink Pepper

MAKES 4 SERVINGS

2 lb (1 kg) lean ground pork
¼ cup (50 mL) cubed mild cheddar cheese
2 tbsp (25 mL) honey mustard
1 tbsp (15 mL) ground pink pepper
2 tbsp (25 mL) chopped chives
salt and pepper, to taste
1 pig's stomach lining*
3 tbsp (45 mL) butter
1 shallot**, chopped
½ cup (125 mL) demi-glace sauce** or brown veal stock***
2 tbsp (25 mL) tomato sauce or ketchup

In a bowl, mix together ground pork, mild cheddar, honey mustard, pink pepper and chives. Season with salt and pepper. Shape into small patties. Spread out stomach lining and tightly wrap patties in it. Heat butter in a pan and cook patties for 3 minutes on each side. Then place patties in an ovenproof dish and cook for 4 to 5 minutes at 300 to 325°F (150 to 160°C). Cook shallot in pan used for cooking patties. Add demi-glace sauce or veal stock. Mix in tomato sauce or ketchup and season with salt and pepper, if needed. Cover bottom of individual plates with sauce; add patties directly from oven. This dish can be served with fried new potatoes.

*Also known as caul fat. Before using, soak stomach lining in cold water for 30 minutes
** See glossary
*** You may substitute beef broth or bouillon

Ground pork and caul fat

CHEF'S TIP

Order stomach lining from your butcher about a week ahead of time.

WINE SUGGESTIONS

Very supple and light red wines are good at highlighting the gentle flavor of this dish. The choice is yours: a Bardolino (Veneto), a Côtes du Ventoux (Southeast France) or a Gamy produced in the Touraine region, served slightly chilled (57°F/14°C).

CHEF'S TIP

To make life easier, ask your butcher to split the feet in two lengthwise.

WINE SUGGESTIONS

The texture produced by cooking the feet in bread crumbs makes this a dish to serve with dry and fruity white wines that are refreshingly crisp on the palate. Good selections include Alsace wines (Sylvaner or Pinot Blanc) or a Sauvignon from Chile. Serve at 46 to 50°F (8 to 10°C).

Breaded Pigs' Feet

MAKES 4 SERVINGS

1 onion
1 carrot
2 sprigs fresh thyme
2 bay leaves
1 celery stalk
3 or 4 cloves
4 juniper berries
20 cups (5 L) water
salt and pepper to taste
1 clove garlic, crushed
4 whole pigs' feet cut in half

3 tbsp (45 mL) lard
½ cup (125 mL) bread crumbs
2 tbsp (25 mL) chopped fresh parsley

Peel onion and carrot; cut into pieces. Place in a pot. Add thyme, bay leaves, celery, cloves, juniper berries and water. Season with salt and pepper and add garlic. Wash pigs' feet thoroughly and place in pot. Cook ingredients for 2 hours and 30 minutes to 3 hours, until pigs' feet are well cooked. Add water during cooking to keep feet covered.

Cool cooked feet, cut in two lengthwise (if not already done by butcher) and brush with lard. Mix together bread crumbs and parsley. Cover feet completely with bread crumb mixture. Place in ovenproof dish and cook in a 300°F (150°C) oven for 30 minutes. Serve.

Pigs' feet should not be eaten cold. To reheat, place them in a slow oven or microwave for 3 to 4 minutes.

Old-Fashioned Pigs' Tails

MAKES 4 SERVINGS

2 tbsp (25 mL) vegetable oil
3 onions, chopped
3 tbsp (45 mL) tomato paste
12 pigs' tails, fresh
2 celery stalks, diced
2 leeks, sliced
1 clove garlic, crushed
1 tsp (5 mL) oregano
1 cup (250 mL) dry white wine
2 cups (500 mL) broth of your choice
1 tsp (5 mL) Quatre Épices*
1 tomato, seeded and diced
salt and pepper, to taste

Heat oil in cast-iron pot and sauté onions for 3 to 4 minutes. Add tomato paste, pigs' tails, celery, leeks, garlic and oregano. Add wine and broth. Add Quatre Épices and diced tomato and season with salt and pepper. Add enough water to cover. Cover and cook in a 375°F (190°C) oven for hour and 15 minutes. Remove pot from oven and continue simmering on top of stove, uncovered. Let cooking liquid evaporate gradually until there is just enough to serve with tails. Total cooking time should be 2 hours and 15 minutes. Serve tails and broth in soup plates. Tails can be eaten as is, or with baked potatoes, carrots or braised cabbage.

See glossary

CHEF'S TIP

If you want to eat this dish au gratin, place pigs' tails in an ovenproof dish and brush with olive oil. Sprinkle with a mixture of bread crumbs, herbs and chopped garlic. Cook in 425°F (220°C) oven for 5 to 6 minutes. Do not set oven at broil or crumbs will burn.

WINE SUGGESTIONS

The logical choice to match the tomato and flavoring agents in this country-style recipe is an earthy wine with a fruity, vanilla like or spicy aroma. Consider Coteaux du Languedoc, La Clape or Pic Saint-Loup when making your choice.

Hock

CHEF'S TIP

Use cooking liquid as a base for soups or use it to cook vegetables.

WINE SUGGESTIONS

This dish calls for a dense, rich and tannic red wine. Though a bit rustic, a Pécharmant, Marcillac or Côtes du Marmandais (Southwest France) would be fine. A Fitou (Languedoc) is also a good choice.

Winter Potato and Pork Stew

MAKES 4 SERVINGS

4 lb (2 kg) pork hocks
1 onion
1 carrot, cut into pieces
1 stalk celery
1 tomato, seeded and finely chopped
1 bouquet garni*
6 cups (1.5 L) beef broth
salt and pepper, to taste
1 tbsp (15 mL) tomato paste
½ cup (125 mL) flour
8 potatoes
2 tbsp (25 mL) chopped fresh parsley

Place hocks in a large pot, blanch for 2 to 3 minutes and drain. In a large skillet brown with onion, carrot, celery, tomato and bouquet garni. Add broth, season with salt and pepper and add tomato paste. Cook over medium heat for 2 hours. Remove skin and part of fat from hocks, leaving meat attached to the bone. Gradually add broth to flour until mixture has a smooth consistency. Thicken cooking liquid with flour mixture. Peel potatoes, cut in half and cook in the cooking liquid for 20 to 30 minutes, over medium heat. Place hocks on plates and surround with potatoes. Serve with cooking liquid and fresh parsley.

* See glossary

Three-Hour Braised Pork Roast

MAKES 6 TO 8 SERVINGS

3 tbsp (45 mL) butter
1 onion, chopped
3 lb (1.5 kg) pork roast, cut from leg or loin
salt and pepper, to taste
½ pumpkin, cut into chunks
12 mushrooms, whole or sliced
4 cloves garlic, whole
10 pearl onions
2 fresh tomatoes, crushed
2 tbsp (25 mL) chopped fresh parsley
4 cups (1 L) beef or chicken broth
2 tbsp (25 mL) chopped green onions

Heat butter in a roasting pan and cook onions for 1 to 2 minutes, until transparent. Brown roast on all sides and season with salt and pepper. Add pumpkin, mushrooms, garlic, pearl onions, tomato and parsley. Add broth, cover and cook in a 350°F (180°C) oven for one hour. Lower oven temperature to 250°F (120°C) and season with salt and pepper again, if needed. Cook for 1 hour, then lower temperature to 175°F (80°C). Uncover and cook for 1 more hour. Remove roast from oven after 3 hours of cooking, place on serving dish and decorate with garnish of chopped green onion. Roast can be served with sautéed new potatoes or fresh vegetables.

Leg tip roast, boneless

CHEF'S TIP

This slow-cooked Cajun dish originated in Louisiana. It's the ideal choice for hearty eaters.

WINE SUGGESTIONS

Robust supple red wines or dry rosés should be served with this Cajun pork roast dish. Select a Rhône Valley wine such as a red or rosé Côtes du Ventoux or Coteaux du Tricastin or opt for a Tavel. A Corbières rosé (Languedoc) or any of a variety of rosés from Chili are equally good choices.

* or boneless shoulder butt roast, or boneless leg outside roast; or boneless rib-end roast

Ground pork*

CHEF'S TIP

To prevent splattering when frying these sausage (which can also be boiled), pierce them and refrigerate for 30 minutes. Or cook them in the oven and serve with the sauce of your choice. The sausages can also be frozen.

WINE SUGGESTIONS

The tomatoes and tomato sauce make this a colorful dish, worthy of a robust but fruity red wine. Choose a Pécharmant (Bergerac region) or a Barbera d'Alba and serve at 64°F (18°C).

* or jowl or belly, put through a meat grinder

Pork, Cheese and Sun-Dried Tomato Sausages

MAKES 4 SERVINGS

1 lb (500 g) lean ground pork
½ cup (125 mL) cheddar cheese, cut into very small chunks
3 slices sun-dried tomato, finely minced
1 egg
1 clove garlic, finely minced
2 tbsp (25 mL) chopped fresh parsley
¼ tsp (1 mL) cinnamon
¼ tsp (1 mL) nutmeg
salt and pepper, to taste
3 tbsp (25 mL) tomato sauce
5 feet (1.5 m) Toulouse sausage casing*, (1-1¼ in / 30-32 mm size)

Mix together all ingredients, except casing and tomato sauce, until a smooth consistency is obtained. Add tomato sauce and mix thoroughly. Slip casing onto end of funnel tube and knot the end. Place meat mixture in funnel. Fill casing and knot or tie at regular intervals to make sausages that are 6 in (15 cm) long.

This recipe lets you make your own sausages and cook them whatever way you like.

* Order Toulouse sausage casing from your butcher about a week ahead of planned cooking time. Before using, soak it in cold water for 30 minutes.

Head Cheese à la Mollé

MAKES 6 TO 8 SERVINGS

2 lb (1 kg) pigs' head, feet, jowl or hocks
or a combination of all, mixed
2 carrots, chopped
1 onion
1 leek
2 cloves garlic, chopped
1 bouquet garni*
salt and pepper, to taste
¼ tsp (1 mL) nutmeg (optional)
4 green onion stems, sliced or chopped

Rinse pork pieces and place in a large pot with carrots, onion, leek, chopped garlic and bouquet garni. Cover with water. Bring to a boil, cover and cook for 1 hour and 30 minutes to 2 hours. When meat falls away from bone, remove from heat and cut off any excess fat. Cut meat into pieces and place in a bowl. Strain cooking liquid and pour on meat. Season with salt and pepper. Add nutmeg, if desired, and place mixture in a terrine dish. Sprinkle with green onion and refrigerate for at least 4 hours.

This head cheese can be served as is, with a vinaigrette or with a yogurt-based sauce. For a more gelatinlike consistency, add a package of gelatin. Usually, the gelatin produced by cooking the head is enough to obtain the desired consistency. If you are using a combination of meat be sure to include some feet for the gelatin they will provide.

* See glossary

Jowl

CHEF'S TIP

Head cheese, a well-liked and old-fashioned dish, is also known as brawn in some areas.

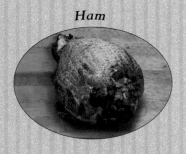

WINE SUGGESTIONS

Tender white wines with a very light aroma are ideally suited to this smooth dish. An Île de Beauté Chardonnay (Corsica), a Vin de Pays d'Oc (Languedoc) or a wine from Chile are your best options. If your budget permits, try a Saint-Véran and other Pouilly-Vinzelles offerings (Burgundy, Mâcon region).

Ham Steaks with Pumpkin and Yellow Pepper Sauce

MAKES 4 SERVINGS

4 steaks of ham from a bone-in cut, 6 oz (175 g) each,
about ½ in (1 cm) thick
½ pumpkin
1 yellow pepper
2 tbsp (25 mL) olive oil
salt and pepper, to taste
¼ cup (50 mL) whipping cream (35%)
½ tsp (2 mL) nutmeg
water or chicken broth, if necessary
12 snow peas
3 tbsp (45 mL) vegetable oil

Place ham slices in a large stock pot to steam through over very low heat. Peel and cut pumpkin into pieces and slice yellow pepper. In a pan, heat olive oil and cook pumpkin and pepper for 4 to 5 minutes. Season with salt and pepper. Add cream and cook for 3 to 4 minutes longer. Blend mixture in food processor, add nutmeg and set aside. If sauce is too thick, dilute with a small amount of water or chicken stock. Cut ends off snow peas, string and sauté in vegetable oil for 1 to 2 minutes. Cover bottom of plates with sauce, add ham and garnish with snow peas and some reserved julienned pepper.

Succulent Stuffings

Tantalizing combinations!

Boneless chops, for stuffing

WINE SUGGESTIONS

Ginger and apricots go well with an aromatic white wine that's dry but firm. Choose a California Chardonnay with just the right amount of oak flavor. More expensive alternatives are a white Châteauneuf-du-Pape or, better yet, the incomparable Condrieu (Rhône Valley).

Pork Chops with Citrus Apricot Stuffing

MAKES 4 SERVINGS

6 dried apricots
1 piece of fresh ginger about 1 in (2.5 cm)
4 split boneless pork chops (butterfly-style)
3 tbsp (45 mL) vegetable oil
salt and pepper, to taste
3 tbsp (45 mL) brown sugar
2 shallots*
½ cup (125 ml) brown veal stock**
2 tbsp (25 mL) whipping cream (35%)
2 tbsp (25 mL) chopped green onion

Coarsely chop dried apricots; do not mince. Sliver fresh ginger. Mix together apricots and ginger. Stuff chops with part of apricot-ginger mixture. In a skillet, heat vegetable oil and brown chops for about 2 to 3 minutes on each side. Season with salt and pepper. Place chops in an ovenproof dish. Add brown sugar, return to heat and cook until a caramel color is obtained. Add shallots and remaining apricot-ginger mixture. Cook for 2 to 3 minutes.

Combine veal stock and cream, mix until smooth and pour sauce on chops. Season with salt and pepper. Place chops in a 325°F (160°C) oven, cover and cook for 4 minutes. Cover bottom of plates with sauce, add chops and sprinkle with green onion. Serve with vegetables or buttered noodles.

Select pork chops that are 1 to 1¼ in (2 to 3 cm) thick and ask your butcher to split them for stuffing.

* See glossary
** You may substitute beef broth or bouillon

Small Pasta Shells with Pork Filling

MAKES 4 SERVINGS

½ lb (250 g) small pasta shells or cannelloni
½ lb (250 g) ground pork
4 slices sun-dried tomatoes, chopped
1 clove garlic, finely minced
¼ cup (50 mL) spicy Diana sauce*
2 tbsp (25 mL) Taleggio cheese, grated
salt and pepper, to taste

Sauce
3 tbsp (45 mL) olive oil
1 cup (250 mL) dry white wine
2 Italian plum tomatoes
1 onion
salt and pepper, to taste
2 cloves garlic, whole
6 shredded fresh basil leaves

Cook pasta in boiling salted water for 6 to 7 minutes and rinse with cold water. Mix together pork, sun-dried tomatoes, garlic, Diana sauce and cheese. Season with salt and pepper. Using a fork or pastry bag, fill pasta and place in ovenproof dish.

Sauce
Add olive oil, white wine, tomatoes, onion and garlic cloves to pasta. Season with salt and pepper and bake in a 325°F (160°C) oven for 20 minutes. Remove from oven and sprinkle with basil leaves.

* See glossary

Ground pork

CHEF'S TIP

Taleggio cheese is available in Italian grocery stores, but Gruyère is a good substitute. The same recipe can be used with cannelloni.

WINE SUGGESTIONS

Full-bodied red Italian wines are the best choice for this fairly spicy dish. A Cannonau di Sardegna or a traditional Chianti Classico, both known for their high acidity and good tannin structure, are sure to please discriminating gourmets.

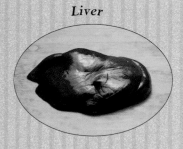

CHEF'S TIP

*Order stomach lining from
your butcher about a week
ahead of time.*

WINE SUGGESTIONS

*Since this recipe combines
liver, fennel and wine, you
should look for an aromatic
and slightly spicy red wine,
fairly robust with fruity
notes, to accompany it. Good
choices include a Rioja
Reserva (Spain), a Cabernet
Sauvignon or a Shiraz from
Australia. Serve at between
57 and 64°F (16 and 18°C).*

Stuffed Liver

MAKES 6 TO 8 SERVINGS

2 to 3 lb (1 to 1.5 kg) pork liver in a piece
3 tbsp (45 mL) butter
½ cup (125 mL) sliced mushrooms
salt and pepper, to taste
¼ lb (125 g) ground pork
1 egg
1 tsp (5 mL) chopped chives
1 pig's stomach lining*
2 tbsp (25 mL) olive oil
1 tsp (5 mL) chopped pili-pili pepper or dried chili pepper
2 cups (500 mL) red wine
½ cup (125 mL) chicken stock
2 fennel bulbs

Remove skin covering liver or ask your butcher to remove it. Make a
large incision in the middle of the liver. Melt butter in a pan and sauté
mushrooms for 2 to 3 minutes. Season with salt and pepper and set aside.
In a bowl, mix together ground pork, mushrooms and egg. Add chives
and season with salt and pepper. Place stuffing mixture in center of liver.
Wrap liver in stomach lining.

Heat olive oil in an ovenproof dish and brown liver for 1 to 2 minutes.
Sprinkle with pili-pili or chili pepper. Add red wine, previously heated
and flambéed to remove alcohol content. Add bouillon and chopped fennel. Place in oven, cover and cook for 30 minutes. Remove cover, season
with salt and pepper and cook for 15 to 20 minutes longer. Serve as is
with broth.

Also known as caul fat. Before using, soak stomach lining in cold water for 30 minutes

Paupiettes à la Forestière

MAKES 4 SERVINGS

8 small stuffed paupiettes*
salt and pepper, to taste
3 tbsp (45 mL) butter
1 shallot**, chopped
½ lb (250 g) white mushrooms, cleaned and chopped
1 carrot, sliced into rounds
3 tbsp (45 mL) sherry or port
1 tsp (5 mL) garlic, chopped
1 cup (250 mL) brown or thickened veal stock***
4 green onion sprigs, chopped

Season paupiettes lightly with salt and pepper. Melt butter in a pan and brown paupiettes for 2 to 3 minutes on each side. Add shallot, mushrooms and carrot. Cook mixture for 2 minutes, then add sherry or port. Add chopped garlic and veal stock. Cover and cook over medium heat for about 2 minutes. Remove cover and cook until sauce begins to reduce. Sprinkle with green onion. Place paupiettes in a serving dish and cover with sauce.

For a cream sauce, just before serving add 3 tbsp (45 mL) whipping cream (35%) and season with salt and pepper, if desired.

* *Paupiettes are available from your butcher, or make you own by adding a ground pork stuffing, seasoned to your taste, to leg cutlets*
** *See glossary*
*** *You may substitute beef broth or bouillon*

Paupiettes

CHEF'S TIP

Paupiettes are also available wrapped in a strip of fat to prevent them from drying out during cooking.

WINE SUGGESTIONS

The stuffing, sherry and mushrooms give this dish the kind of flavoring that calls for a vigorous red wine with subtle tannins. Select wines from the Southwest of France, such as a Gaillac, a Bergerac or a Buzet. Serve at 41°F (15°C).

*Ground pork**

CHEF'S TIP

Pumpkin and orange go extremely well with pork.

WINE SUGGESTIONS

Riesling is the perfect match for this dish's citrus and spicy notes. Alsace wines or wines from Germany, particularly Moselles, are an excellent choice.

* or a belly cut, put through a meat grinder

Pork and Parsley-Stuffed Pumpkin with Orange Sauce

MAKES 4 SERVINGS

1 small pumpkin
½ lb (250 g) lean ground pork
¼ cup (50 mL) chopped fresh parsley
1 tsp (5 mL) ground ginger
⅓ cup (75 mL) tomato juice
1 tbsp (15 mL) curry powder
salt and pepper, to taste

Orange Sauce
¼ cup (50 mL) sugar
2 tbsp (25 mL) wine vinegar
½ cup (125 mL) orange juice
⅓ cup (50 mL) veal stock or beef or chicken broth
2 tbsp (25 mL) cornstarch
salt and pepper, to taste

Cut top off pumpkin and reserve. Using a spoon, hollow out pumpkin, leaving a ½ in (1 cm) layer. In a bowl, mix together pork, parsley, ginger, tomato juice and curry. Season with salt and pepper. Stuff pumpkin with mixture and replace top. Pour ½ cup (125 mL) of water into an oven-proof dish, place pumpkin in dish and cook in a 325°F (160°C) oven for 35 to 40 minutes.

Sauce
Cook sugar and vinegar until a caramel mixture is obtained. Add enough orange juice and veal stock or broth to give caramel mixture a golden color. Cook until reduced by half. Mix cornstarch with 2 tbsp (25 mL) water, add to sauce and thicken to desired consistency. Season with salt and pepper. Place pumpkin on a serving dish and surround with sauce.

Ground Pork, Tomato and Herb Pizza

MAKES 4 SERVINGS

3 tbsp (45 mL) vegetable oil
4 pizza crusts, 6 in (15 cm) diameter
2 tbsp (25 mL) olive oil
1 onion, finely chopped
1 pepper, finely chopped
2 lb (1 kg) lean ground pork
salt and pepper, to taste
⅓ cup (75 mL) spicy Diana sauce*
1 tsp (5 mL) garlic, minced
1 tsp (5 mL) savory
1 tsp (5 mL) oregano
olive oil in sufficient quantity to brush tomatoes
2 fresh tomatoes
1 tbsp (15 mL) Herbes de Provence*, dried
grated Parmesan, to taste (optional)

Brush pizza crusts with olive oil and set aside. In a pan, heat olive oil, add onion and pepper and cook for 2 to 3 minutes. Add ground pork and cook over medium heat for 3 to 4 minutes. Season with salt and pepper. Add Diana sauce, garlic, savory and oregano, cover and cook over very low heat for 15 to 20 minutes. Slice tomatoes, brush with olive oil and sprinkle with Herbes de Provence. Let sauce cool, spread generous amount on bottom of pizza crusts and add herbed tomato slices. Place pizza on a baking sheet and cook in a moderate oven for 7 to 10 minutes. Sprinkle with grated Parmesan, if desired.

See glossary

Ground pork

CHEF'S TIP

You can also use a belly cut that has been put through a meat grinder.

WINE SUGGESTIONS

Look for simple reds or rosés that are sufficiently aromatic to match the flavors of the sauce and condiments used in this dish. A Faugères or Saint-Chinian (Languedoc) or a Cannonau (Grenache de Sardigne) will fit the bill nicely. Serve at about 60°F (16°C).

Ground pork

CHEF'S TIP

This dish takes a light touch and a bit of work, but it's well worth the trouble!

WINE SUGGESTIONS

Do as the Italians do: enjoy these zucchini blossoms with a light, fruity and supple red wine, such as the Merlot del Piave (Veneto) or a Dolcetto d'Alba (Piedmont). Serve at 60°F (16°C).

Zucchini Blossoms with Ricotta and Sun-Dried Tomato Filling

MAKES 2 SERVINGS

5 oz (150 g) lean ground pork
¼ cup (50 mL) ricotta
5 slices of sun-dried tomatoes
1 clove garlic, chopped
1 tbsp (15 mL) chopped fresh coriander*
3 tbsp (45 mL) whipping cream (35%)
1 egg
3 tbsp (45 mL) sherry
salt and pepper, to taste
6 zucchini blossoms
2 tbsp (25 mL) olive oil
1 package frozen spinach, 10 oz (284 g), chopped
2 cups (500 mL) chicken broth

Mix together ground pork and ricotta. Add two dried tomato slices, garlic, coriander, cream, egg and sherry. Season with salt and pepper. Gently clean zucchini blossoms, open and, using a pastry bag, fill with meat mixture. Close petals. Heat olive oil and cook chopped spinach for 1 minute. Add remaining tomato slices, cut into julienne strips. Place stuffed flowers in an ovenproof dish, add chicken broth and cook, covered, in a moderate oven, at 325 to 350°F (160 to 180°C), for 5 to 7 minutes. Place zucchini blossoms in a serving dish and top with spinach mixture.

* See glossary

Pork-Stuffed Vegetables

MAKES 4 SERVINGS

¾ lb (375 g) ground pork
1 tomato, seeded and diced
2 tbsp (25 mL) chili sauce
1 shallot*, chopped
3 tbsp (45 mL) fresh parsley
3 tbsp (45 mL) basil
2 medium zucchinis
4 medium tomatoes
1 pepper, halved lengthwise, seeded
3 tbsp (45 mL) olive oil
1 onion, finely chopped
4 Italian plum tomatoes, crushed
1 clove garlic, chopped
1 tsp (5 mL) oregano
1 tbsp (15 mL) sugar
1 cup (250 mL) tomato or clam and tomato (Clamato) juice
salt and pepper, to taste

Mix together ground pork, tomato, chili sauce, shallot, parsley and basil. Season with salt and pepper. Using a melon baller, hollow out zucchinis to form a boat shape. Use the same method to hollow out tomatoes. Seed pepper.

In a pan, heat oil, add onion and cook over medium heat for 3 minutes. Add crushed tomatoes, garlic and oregano and cook for 2 to 3 minutes. Add sugar and tomato or Clamato juice. Season with salt and pepper. Cover and cook slowly for 15 to 20 minutes. Remove cover, reduce sauce and put mixture through blender. Set aside.

Stuff hollowed-out vegetables with filling and place in a deep oven-proof dish. Reduce sauce to desired consistency. Add sauce to vegetables, add 1 cup (250 mL) water and cook in a 350°F (180°C) oven for 15 to 20 minutes.

* See glossary

Ground pork *

CHEF'S TIP

Zucchinis and peppers can be blanched in boiling water for 1 minute.

WINE SUGGESTIONS

These beautifully colorful and flavorful vegetables go well with dry and vigorous rosés or fruity reds served well chilled. Choose Minervois, Corbières or Côtes du Roussillon rosés, or reds featuring the same appellations, produced using a carbonic maceration technique (fruity and lighter).

* or belly cut, put through a meat grinder

CHEF'S TIP

You can reheat the pears in a microwave oven, at low heat, for 2 minutes.

WINE SUGGESTIONS

A Côtes du Frontonnais rosé or a Bordeaux rosé, served well chilled (46°F / 8°C) is an elegant accompaniment for this unusual dish.

Pears Stuffed with Ground Pork

MAKES 4 SERVINGS

8 Bosc or Anjou pears
1 lemon
½ lb (250 g) ground pork, lean
2 tbsp (25 mL) olive oil
1 egg
¼ cup (50 mL) grated cheddar cheese
1 clove garlic, finely minced
1 tbsp (15 mL) chopped chives
1 tbsp (15 mL) grated ginger

1 slice of sun-dried tomato, finely minced
3 tbsp (45 mL) balsamic vinegar
salt and pepper, to taste
3 tbsp (45 mL) orange juice
2 fresh tomatoes, seeded and diced
½ cup (125 mL) whipping cream (35%)
½ tsp (2 mL) nutmeg

Peel pears and rub with lemon to prevent discoloring. Cut top off pears and hollow out with a melon baller, removing pulp and core. In a bowl, mix together ground pork, olive oil and egg. Add cheese, garlic, chives, ginger, minced dried tomatoes and balsamic vinegar. Season lightly with salt and pepper. Fill pears with mixture and place in a ceramic or glass ovenproof dish. Add 250 mL (1 cup) water and orange juice. Cover and bake in a 325°F (160°C) oven for 15 to 20 minutes. Remove pears and put cooking juices and diced fresh tomatoes through food processor. Add cream to puréed mixture and heat in a pan, cooking for 3 to 4 minutes, until thickened. Add nutmeg and season with salt and pepper again, if necessary. Gently reheat pears, place in dish and surround with tomato-cream sauce. Serve immediately.

Blueberry-Stuffed Pork Roast with Cream Sauce

MAKES 6 SERVINGS

3 lb (1.5 kg) belly or half-belly
pork roast, fat removed
3 tbsp (45 mL) butter
1 onion, chopped
1 lb (500 g) lean ground pork
1 clove garlic, chopped
salt and pepper, to taste
1 egg
1 cup (250 mL) blueberries
½ cup (125 mL) cider
1 pig's stomach lining*
1 tbsp (15 mL) dried herbs
2 tbsp (25 mL) vegetable oil

4 cups (1 L) chicken or beef broth

Cream Sauce
1 shallot, chopped**
2 tbsp (25 mL) butter
3 tbsp (45 mL) white Noilly Prat
(French) vermouth
½ cup (125 mL) whipping cream
(35%)
1 cup (250 mL) veal stock or beef
broth
1 tbsp (15 mL) hot mustard
salt and pepper, to taste

Spread roast and slit sides. Heat butter and sauté onions for 4 to 5 minutes, until transparent. Place onions in a bowl and mix together with ground pork and garlic until well blended. Season with salt and pepper. Add egg, half of blueberries and cider. Place stuffing in center of meat and roll meat around stuffing. Wrap in stomach lining and sprinkle with herbs. Brush a pan with vegetable oil and brown pork. Add broth. Place in a 350°F (180°C) oven and cook for 1 hour and 45 minutes to 2 hours, basting often.

Cream Sauce

Sauté shallot in butter for 1 to 2 minutes; do not brown. Add white vermouth and reduce to three-quarters, then add cream and veal stock. Reduce to half. Add hot mustard and season with salt and pepper. At the last minute, add remaining blueberries.

Slice and serve with sauce, along with sautéed zucchini or your choice of vegetable.

*Also known as caul fat. Before using, soak stomach lining in cold water for 30 minutes

** See glossary

Belly cut

CHEF'S TIP

Order stomach lining from your butcher about a week ahead of time. Before using, soak it in cold water for 30 minutes.
If stomach lining is unavailable, secure the roast with string.

WINE SUGGESTIONS

The color of the berries, the smooth cream sauce and the overall texture of this dish go very well with a fruity and supple red wine. Make your selection a Merlot from Languedoc (Vin de Pays), Frioul (Grave del Friuli, Colli Orientali del Fruili), or choose a Rosso di Montalcino (Tuscany) or a tender Chilean Cabernet Sauvignon a few years old.

Ground pork *

CHEF'S TIP

*You can prepare this recipe
using other small
vegetables — peppers in
a variety of colors,
eggplant, zucchini or any
other type of squash.*

WINE SUGGESTIONS

*The colorful peppers and
tomatoes and wonderful
thyme and garlic accents in
this dish call for a dry and
fruity rosé. Select a Côtes de
Provence, Bandol
(Provence) or Côtes du
Rhône rosé and remember
to serve your wine
well chilled.*

* or belly cut, put through
a meat grinder*

Yellow and Red Peppers with Fresh Thyme Stuffing

MAKES 2 SERVINGS

½ cup (125 mL) lean ground pork
1 egg
1 clove garlic, very finely minced
1 slice sun-dried tomato, very finely minced
½ tsp (2 mL) fresh thyme
salt and pepper, to taste
1 yellow pepper
1 red pepper
½ cup (125 mL) chicken stock

In a bowl, mix together ground pork, egg, garlic, sun-dried tomato and fresh thyme. Season with salt and pepper. Cut top off peppers and seed. Stuff with meat mixture and place in an ovenproof dish. Bring chicken stock to a boil and add to ovenproof dish. Bake in a 375°F (190°C) oven for 15 to 17 minutes. Turn oven off and let rest for 5 minutes. Serve immediately, in broth.

International Dishes

Olé!

Caramel Pork Cubes and Chinese Noodles

MAKES 4 SERVINGS

1 package Chinese noodles, 7 oz (200 g)
3 tbsp (45 mL) vegetable oil
1 lb (500 g) pork cubes, cut from loin or sirloin
½ cup (125 mL) sugar
¼ cup (50 mL) orange or clementine juice
3 tbsp (45 mL) Chinese oyster sauce
3 tbsp (45 mL) rice vinegar
1 tsp (5 mL) ground ginger
salt and pepper, to taste
2 tbsp (25 mL) chopped fresh parsley or fresh coriander*

Cook noodles in boiling salted water for 2 to 3 minutes. In a wok, heat oil and stir-fry pork cubes for 2 to 3 minutes, until browned. Remove cubes and drain to remove any fat.

In the same wok, cook sugar and orange juice until mixture is a pale caramel color. Remove from heat and stir in oyster sauce, rice vinegar and ginger. If too thick, dilute caramel mixture with 4 tbsp (60 mL) water. When sauce is smooth and creamy, add meat cubes and stir-fry for 2 to 3 minutes longer. Season with salt and pepper. Add precooked noodles to sauce while very hot and heat through. Make a bed of noodles and place pork cubes in center; cover with sauce and sprinkle with parsley or coriander.

* See glossary

Cubes for kabobs

CHEF'S TIP

Chinese cuisine makes extensive use of pork.

WINE SUGGESTIONS

This exotic dish and its unusual caramel sauce are ideally suited to a medium-dry white wine with a touch of acidity. Choose a German wine from the Moselle, Rheingau or Rheinpfalz regions and serve it well chilled (46°F/8°C).

WINE SUGGESTIONS

Dry, vigorous and refreshing rosés go well with this exotic blend of ingredients. Select a rosé from Italy, Spain or the South of France, wines that are dry and have a slight bite, and serve well chilled.

Chinese Stir Fry

MAKES 4 SERVINGS

3 tbsp (45 mL) soya oil
1 onion, minced
4 sliced zucchinis
16 snow peas
1 tomato, seeded and chopped
½ green pepper, sliced
1 lb (500 g) pork strips cut from loin or leg
¼ cup (50 mL) Chinese oyster sauce
2 tbsp (25 mL) rice vinegar
1 tbsp (15 mL) soy sauce
1 tsp (5 mL) grated ginger
2 tbsp (25 mL) chopped fresh coriander*
¼ tsp (1 mL) dried chili pepper
salt (optional)

Prepare vegetables. In a pan or wok, heat soya oil. Over high heat, stir-fry all vegetables, except chili pepper, for 2 minutes. Set aside vegetables. In the same pan or wok, without adding any fat, cook pork strips for 2 to 3 minutes. Add oyster sauce, rice vinegar and soy sauce. Cook for 2 minutes, over very low heat. Return vegetables to pan or wok, add ginger and mix well. Add coriander and chili pepper. Season with salt, if desired.

* See glossary

Fajitas and Salsa

MAKES 4 SERVINGS

3 tbsp (45 mL) olive oil
1 onion, chopped
1 pepper, seeded and sliced
1 tomato, seeded and diced
1 clove garlic, minced
¼ cup (50 mL) chili sauce
1 tbsp (15 mL) Worcestershire sauce
½ tsp (2 mL) Tabasco sauce
salt and pepper, to taste
1 lb (500 g) pork strips, cut from the loin or leg
2 tbsp (25 mL) vegetable oil
8 flour tortillas
8 lettuce leaves
4 fresh or canned tomatoes

Heat olive oil and sauté onion, pepper and tomato. Cook for 5 to 7 minutes, then add garlic, chili sauce, Worcestershire sauce and Tabasco sauce. Season with salt and pepper, cover and, over low heat, reduce mixture for 10 minutes. Remove cover and continue reducing until liquid has evaporated.

Season strips with salt and pepper. In a nonstick pan, heat vegetable oil and sauté strips for 2 to 3 minutes. Add strips to sauce, season with salt and pepper again, if necessary, then let cool. Fold fajitas into cone shapes, seam side under, and fill with meat mixture. Place fajitas in a 375°F (190°C) oven and bake for 4 to 5 minutes, until crispy. Add coarsely shredded lettuce leaves and diced tomatoes.

Strips

CHEF'S TIP

If you wish, cut strips smaller.

WINE SUGGESTIONS

Full-bodied red wines with spicy or slightly woody aromas are an excellent match for these fajitas. A Zinfandel (California), a Cabernet Sauvignon or a Shiraz from Australia and some Cabernet Sauvignon wines from Chili would all be good choices.

Cubes for kabobs

WINE SUGGESTIONS

The ingredients in this recipe combine to produce a marvelous dish, highlighted by the tamari sauce and honey. You're sure to enjoy it along with the almond-paste aroma of dry and fairly supple white wines, such as a Vernaccia di San Gimignano (Tuscany) or a Fiano di Avellino (Campania).

Fricassée with Tamari Sauce and Almonds

MAKES 2 SERVINGS

2 tbsp (25 mL) vegetable oil
½ lb (250 g) pork cubes or strips cut from leg or loin
12 snow peas
1 zucchini, sliced
6 white mushrooms, quartered
1 onion, chopped
3 tbsp (45 mL) tamari* sauce
2 tbsp (25 mL) honey
1 clove garlic, minced
1 tsp (5 mL) grated ginger
salt and pepper, to taste
8 blanched almonds, whole
4 chive leaves, chopped

In a pan, heat oil and cook pork cubes or strips for 2 to 3 minutes. Add snow peas, zucchini, mushrooms and onion. Add tamari sauce. Mix well and add honey, garlic and ginger. Season with salt and pepper. Add almonds, cook for 2 to 3 minutes longer and sprinkle with chives.

* See glossary

Chinese-Style Pork Strips

MAKES 4 SERVINGS

3 tbsp (45 mL) vegetable oil
¾ lb (375 g) pork strips
4 zucchinis
½ cup (125 mL) green beans
6 baby squash or 3 zucchinis
1 red pepper, sliced
6 small pickling cucumbers
2 tbsp (25 mL) tamari* sauce
2 tbsp (25 mL) cornstarch
salt and pepper, to taste
1 tbsp (15 mL) grated ginger
1 package, 1 lb (500 g) chow mein noodles
4 green onions

In a wok, heat vegetable oil and cook strips, zucchinis and beans for 3 minutes. Remove. In the same wok, sauté baby squash or zucchinis, pepper and cucumbers. Add tamari sauce. Mix cornstarch with ¼ cup (50 mL) water. Add mixture and return vegetables and strips to wok. Season with salt and pepper. Add ginger, mix well and set aside. Cook noodles in boiling salted water for 5 to 6 minutes and rinse under cold water. Cut up noodles and add to wok mixture, stirring well. Season with salt and pepper, sprinkle with green onion stems and serve.

* See glossary

Strips

CHEF'S TIP

You can use long Chinese green beans or vegetables such as bok choy or Chinese cabbage.

WINE SUGGESTIONS

The Chinese-inspired ingredients and ginger in this recipe call for dry or medium-dry white wines with a fair amount of acidity. Select a German wine from the Moselle or Rheingau regions or a South African vintage. Remember to serve your wine well chilled (46°F/8°C).

Cubes for kabobs

CHEF'S TIP

Okra, a very gelatinous vegetable, is also called gumbo in some regions.

WINE SUGGESTIONS

Simple but vigorous reds and rosés will get along well with the colors and flavors in this West Indian dish. Impress your guests with a slightly spicy red Zinfandel (California) or a rosé Tavel (Rhône Valley).

Pork Sauté à la Martiniquaise

MAKES 4 SERVINGS

½ lb (250 g) okra
¼ cup (50 mL) vegetable oil
2 white onions, minced
1 lb (500 g) pork cubes, cut from the loin or sirloin
1 pili-pili or jalapeno pepper, coarsely chopped
1 celery stalk, finely diced
2 sprigs Italian parsley
2 cloves garlic, chopped
2 tbsp (45 mL) original Diana sauce*
2 cups (500 mL) veal stock** or chicken broth or ½ package of instant
broth and 3 cups (750 mL) water
2 tomatoes, seeded and chopped
salt and pepper, to taste

Cook okra in boiling salted water for 3 to 4 minutes, then cool under running water and reserve. In a Dutch oven, heat vegetable oil and cook onions and pork for 3 to 4 minutes. Add chopped pepper, celery and Italian parsley leaves. Add garlic, Diana sauce and veal or chicken stock. Add tomatoes, cover and cook for 15 minutes. Remove cover, add okra and season with salt and pepper. Cover and cook over medium heat for 15 minutes. Serve in an earthenware dish, soup tureen or small stoneware pot.

You can garnish this dish with croutons seasoned with garlic or chopped herbs. It can be reheated, but it cannot be frozen because of the okra.

* See glossary
** You may substitute beef broth or bouillon

Pork Roast with Red Kidney Beans

MAKES 6 TO 8 SERVINGS

3 lb (1.5 kg) pork leg tip roast
salt and pepper, to taste
3 tbsp (45 mL) vegetable oil
1 onion, finely chopped
2 tomatoes, seeded and coarsely diced
1 tbsp (15 mL) chili pepper flakes
1 lb (500 g) dried kidney beans, soaked (see note below)
1 bouquet garni*
8 cups (2 L) broth
4 cloves garlic, minced
2 green onions, chopped

Preheat oven to 325°F (160°C). Place meat in roasting pan, season with salt and pepper and brush with vegetable oil. Cook roast for 1 hour to 1 hour and 45 minutes, maximum. Remove from oven and let rest for 5 to 10 minutes. Place diced onion, tomatoes and chili peppers in a cast-iron pot. Add kidney beans, bouquet garni and cover with water. Cook for 5 minutes, until water has almost evaporated completely. Add broth, garlic, green onions and cook for 45 minutes. Remove cover and let cooking juices evaporate for 20 minutes. Slice roast, place on top of kidney beans, cover and cook at low temperature for at least 20 minutes. Sprinkle with chives or chopped green onion and serve in cooking pot.

🌶 Before cooking them, soak the kidney beans in cold water for approximately three hours. Or substitute one 19 oz (540 mL) can of kidney beans drained and rinsed.

* See glossary

Leg tip roast, boneless*

CHEF'S TIP

Depending on the type of beans you use, you may have to increase the amount of broth or water in this recipe.

WINE SUGGESTIONS

For this Louisiana-style pork roast, with its green onion and chili peppers, opt for a robust and relatively mature red wine, such as an 8 to 10 year-old Carmignano or a Brunello di Montalcino (Tuscany). Serve your selection at about 65°F (18°C).

* or rib-end roast, boneless; leg outside roast, boneless; shoulder butt roast, boneless

Ground pork

CHEF'S TIP

Won ton wrappers are available in the produce section of most supermarkets or in Asian grocery stores.

Chinese Pork Won Ton Soup

MAKES 8 TO 10 SERVINGS

½ lb (250 g) lean ground pork
2 tbsp (25 mL) ground ginger
2 tbsp (25 mL) chopped fresh coriander*
2 tbsp (25 mL) Chinese oyster sauce
2 tbsp (25 mL) Hoisin sauce
2 tbsp (25 mL) rice vinegar
salt and pepper, to taste
1 package of won ton wrappers, ½ lb (250 g)

Broth
2 tbsp (25 mL) vegetable oil
2 celery stalks, chopped
1 red pepper, sliced
4 bunches green onions, chopped
8 cups (2 L) beef broth
3 tbsp (45 mL) soy sauce
1 tbsp (15 mL) ground coriander
salt and pepper, to taste

Mix together pork, ginger, fresh coriander, oyster sauce, Hoisin sauce and rice vinegar. Season with salt and pepper, to taste. Spread out won ton wrappers and wet edges slightly. Place filling in center, fold dough into triangles and use fingers to pinch seam closed.

Broth
In a pan, heat vegetable oil and cook celery, pepper and green onions. Add broth, soy sauce and coriander. Boil for 3 to 4 minutes and simmer won tons for 3 to 4 minutes over medium heat. Season with salt and pepper, if desired. Place won tons in deep dishes and add piping-hot broth. Allow 4 to 6 won tons per serving.

* See glossary

Okra and Baby Vegetable Soup

MAKES 4 SERVINGS

3 tbsp (45 mL) vegetable oil
1 onion, chopped
½ cup (125 mL) shredded cabbage
1 tomato, seeded and diced
1 green pepper, seeded and sliced
½ lb (250 g) small pork cubes
½ cup (125 mL) pasta (of your choice,
but small enough to be used for soup)
4 okra, sliced
1 tsp (5 mL) grated fresh ginger
8 cups (2 L) chicken broth
salt and pepper, to taste

In a large pot, heat oil and add onion, cabbage, tomato, pepper and pork cubes. Cook for 3 to 4 minutes. Add pasta, okra, ginger and broth. Season with salt and pepper. Cook over low heat for about 30 minutes. Serve soup piping hot.

You can also spice up this soup in different ways. Add ½ tsp (2 mL) of Chinese five spice powder or ½ tsp (2 mL) of crushed chilies if you like very spicy soups.

Cubes for kabobs

CHEF'S TIP

A meal in itself, this soup can be served with rice.

Strips*

CHEF'S TIP

Remember that overcooking strips will make them tough. You can also grill them or cook them in a nonstick pan, but only until they begin to brown.

Minestrone with Pork Strips

MAKES 4 SERVINGS

¼ cup (50 mL) olive oil
⅓ cup (75 mL) diced carrots
⅓ cup (75 mL) peas
2 tomatoes, seeded and diced
2 tbsp (25 mL) chopped fresh parsley
1 tbsp (15 mL) chopped fresh basil, or 1 tsp (5 mL) dried basil
⅓ cup (75 mL) baby pasta shells
2 tbsp (25 mL) tomato paste
6 cups (1.5 L) chicken stock
salt and pepper, to taste
1 clove garlic, chopped
½ lb (250 g) pork strips
1 tbsp (15 mL) butter or vegetable oil
1 onion, chopped

In a large pot, heat olive oil and add carrots, peas, tomatoes, parsley and basil and sweat vegetables for 3 to 4 minutes. Add pasta and tomato paste and stir well. Cook for 2 to 3 minutes. Add chicken stock, bring to a boil and season with salt and pepper. Cook for 25 to 30 minutes. Five minutes before cooking is completed, add garlic, and season with salt and pepper again. Set aside.

In another pan, cook pork strips and onion in butter or vegetable oil for 2 to 3 minutes and season lightly with salt and pepper. Add meat to soup. Cover and cook gently for 5 minutes, then serve in soup tureen.

If desired, you can garnish the soup with small garlic croutons. For an even more mouthwatering aroma, add a teaspoon of pesto when cooking is completed.

* or fondue meat

Mexican Pork Tacos

MAKES 4 SERVINGS

3 tbsp (45 mL) vegetable oil
1 onion, chopped
½ lb (250 g) lean ground pork
1 tbsp (15 mL) crushed chili peppers
1 clove garlic, chopped
3 tbsp (45 mL) tomato paste
⅓ cup (75 mL) tomato juice
salt and pepper, to taste
½ cup (125 mL) beer
6 lettuce leaves
4 standard or 8 small taco shells
1 tomato, diced
⅓ cup (75 mL) grated mild cheddar cheese, grated (optional)

In a large pan, heat vegetable oil and add onion and pork. Cook over medium heat for 3 to 5 minutes, stirring constantly. Add chili peppers, garlic, tomato paste and tomato juice. Mix well. Cover and cook over very low heat for 25 minutes. Remove cover and stir well. Season with salt and pepper and add beer. Cook over low heat for 15 to 20 minutes. Set aside and let mixture cool once liquid has evaporated. Shred lettuce leaves and garnish bottom of tacos. Add ground pork, diced tomato and, if desired, grated cheese.

Ground pork

CHEF'S TIP

This mixture can also be used to fill crêpes or pita bread. Although a little spicy, it makes a good lunchtime meal for children. To make it milder, add less of the crushed chilies or eliminate them completely.

Leg tip roast,

boneless

CHEF'S TIP

Dried mushrooms are available in Asian grocery stores and many supermarkets.

WINE SUGGESTIONS

Red and white wines go equally well with this exotic dish, as long as your selection is supple, fruity and vigorous. Tokay Pinot Gris (Alsace) or Châteauneuf-du-Pape (Rhône Valley) are fairly robust whites. Côte de Nuits-Villages (Burgundy) or Saint-Joseph (Rhône Valley) are fruity and delicate reds.

Roast Pork Slices with Chinese Black Mushrooms

MAKES 4 TO 6 SERVINGS

2 lb (1 kg) leg tip roast
salt and pepper, to taste
¼ cup (50 mL) vegetable oil
2 cups (500 mL) dried Chinese black mushrooms
3 tbsp (45 mL) chopped fresh coriander*, or
½ tsp (2 mL) ground coriander
1 clove garlic, chopped
3 tbsp (45 mL) Chinese oyster sauce
½ cup (125 mL) brown veal stock or beef broth

Season roast with salt and pepper and place in a roasting pan. Rub roast with half of vegetable oil and roast for 1 hour to 1 hour and 15 minutes, at 325°F (160°C). Turn oven off and let rest for 15 minutes, then cut into slices ½ in (1 cm) thick. Cook mushrooms in boiling water for 10 minutes, drain and let cool. Heat remaining vegetable oil in a pan or wok and sauté mushrooms. Add coriander, garlic, oyster sauce and veal stock or beef broth. Cook for 2 to 3 minutes and season with salt and pepper. Add pork slices to sauce and serve.

* See glossary

Glossary

Aged cheese: A term used to describe a cheese that has been ripened for several weeks, even several months, in contrast to a fresh cheese.

Baby squash: A very small variety of squash also known as patty pan.

Bacon: A part of the pork belly that has already been cured and smoked.

Bain-marie (cook in a bain-marie): A process that consists of adding boiling water to a receptacle and placing inside it a smaller receptacle containing the food to be cooked or heated. Also called a double boiler.

Balsamic vinegar: A wine vinegar that in some instances is aged for up to 25 years. One of the best balsamic vinegars is produced in Modena, Italy.

Béchamel Sauce: 1 tbsp (15 mL) butter, 2 tsp (10 mL) onion finely minced, 2 tbsp (25 mL) flour, 1½ cups (375 mL) milk, scalded, ⅛ tbsp (1 mL) salt, ⅛ tbsp (1 mL) ground white pepper, pinch of nutmeg. In a saucepan melt the butter and cook onion over very low heat until soft. Stir in the flour and cook the roux until it is foamy and is just beginning to color. Add the milk, whisking constantly, until the mixture is thick and smooth. Stir in remaining ingredients and simmer sauce over very low heat for about 20 minutes or until sauce is reduced to 1 cup (250 mL). Strain sauce before using.

Beurre manié: A blend of equal quantities of very cold butter and flour, used to rectify sauces or to thicken thin ones at the end of the cooking process.

Blanch: To pour boiling water over a meat or vegetable for a few minutes, without cooking the food.

Bocconcini: Fresh mozzarella that has not been aged. The best, stored in brine and rinsed before eating is called *di buffalo* and is made using buffalo milk.

Bouquet garni: A mixture of herbs; usually consists of parsley stems, a celery stalk, a bay leaf and a sprig of thyme. Juniper berries and cloves may also be added.

Clamato: A brand name for a seasoned mixture of tomato and clam juice.

Coconut milk: Milk obtained by pressing the pulp of the coconut. It is also available frozen or in cans (avoid boiling it).

Coriander, fresh: Also known as cilantro.

Cornstarch: A white powder usually mixed with water to use as a thickener. Rice starch is also available.

Deglazing: A process that consists of recovering the caramelized cooking juices by adding a liquid.

Demi-glace: Reducing a veal stock to half its original quantity.

Diana sauce: A highly seasoned tomato sauce (commercial barbecue sauce).

Flageolets: A variety of kidney bean. Flageolets are available dried or precooked.

Flambé: A process that consists of burning off the alcohol in a wine or other alcoholized beverages.

Fresh herbs: If fresh herbs are not available, you may substitute dried herbs, 1 part dried equals 3 parts fresh or 1 tbsp (15 mL) fresh herbs equals 1 tsp (5 mL) dried.

Hass: A variety of avocado, highly sought after because of its superior quality, very fine pulp.

Herbes de Provence: Recipe: Mix the following herbs together: 3 oz (100 g) dried thyme, 3 oz (100 g) dried savory, 2 dried bay leaves, 3 oz (100 g) dried oregano.

Pili-Pili: You may substitute any fresh hot pepper.

Poach: A term usually used in reference to eggs, but also used in connection with other foods; a process that involves cooking a food in a liquid for a relatively short period of time, 3 to 5 minutes. This technique is also used for cooking fish, shellfish and molluscs.

Quatre Épices: Also called "Four Spices" or "Spice Parisienne"; a mixture of cloves, nutmeg, ginger and cinnamon, sold commercially.

Reduce: To cook a sauce until a concentrate is obtained.

Raw ham: Commonly known as prosciutto.

Ricer: A piece of equipment used to break down potato pulp into a ricelike form.

Saffron: Crocus pistils; can be replaced with spigol, a less expensive but very good substitute for saffron.

Seed: To remove the seeds from a vegetable or fruit. Use the tips of your fingers to squeeze seeds out of tomatoes.

Shallot: Onion-like plant with cloves like garlic but of milder flavor. If unavailable you may substitute an equal amount of the white part only of green onions.

Spigol: A substitute for saffron, widely used in Provençal cuisine. Spigol is less expensive than saffron. It is available in grocery stores and gourmet shops.

Strain: To pour a sauce or soup through a strainer, a paper filter or cheesecloth.

Sweat: For example, to sweat leeks. This process consists of placing a food in a fatty substance to make it "sweat," or give up its water. Moderate heat prevents the food from browning.

Swiss chard: A vegetable belonging to the celery family. Most people eat only the ribs of the Swiss chard, but its leaves are edible as well.

Tamari: Soy sauce.

Thicken: To make a sauce or a soup thicker by adding a starch, a roux or a small quantity of beurre manié. A mixture containing an egg yolk and milk can also be used for thickening.

Wok: A cooking pan used in Asian cuisine and shaped like a half-moon. Traditionally made of metal or cast iron, woks are now available in a nonstick format as well.

Worcestershire (sauce): A sauce used mainly in cocktails and cold sauces, and sometimes added to marinades and sauces to add flavor.

$\mathcal{R}$ecipe Index

Blanquette of Pork and Green Apples, 96

Blueberry-Stuffed Pork Roast with Cream Sauce, 197

Braised Pork Chops with Cabbage and Dried Apricots, 142

Braised Pork Chops with Green Flageolet Beans, 41

Braised Rack of Pork with Pearl Onions and Apricots, 100

Breaded Pigs' Feet, 162

Buckwheat Crêpes with Ground Pork and Spinach Filling, 150

Caramel Pork Cubes and Chinese Noodles, 203

Chinese Pork Won Ton Soup, 216

Chinese Stir Fry, 204

Chinese-Style Pork Strips, 211

Chops with Scallops, 78

Cocktail Meatballs and Plantains, 122

Cold After-School Sandwich, 28

Cold Roast Pork, Radicchio and Mango Salad, 62

Cold Roast with Orange-Marinated Cabbage, 130

Cordon Bleu Chops with Demi-Glace Sauce, 107

Couscous Semolina with Spicy Meatballs, 31

Country Style Omelette, 157

Crisp Herbed Spareribs, 81

Curry Coconut Steaks, 66

Fajitas and Salsa, 207

Fresh Rosemary Kabobs with Grainy Mustard, 34

Fricassée of Pork Kidneys and Mushrooms, 115

Fricassée with Tamari Sauce and Almonds, 208

Gratin of Pork Strips and Onions, 46

Grilled Chops and Olives, 42

Ground Pork and Mozzarella Lasagna, 50

Ground Pork Patties with Thyme and Nuts, 45

Ground Pork, Tomato and Gruyère Pie, 119

Ground Pork, Tomato and Herb Pizza, 189

Ham and Sausage Kabobs with Rice, 38

Ham Steaks with Pumpkin and Yellow Pepper Sauce, 174

Head Cheese à la Mollé, 173

Kabobs with Sesame Seeds, 37

Lentil Salad with Vegetables and Pork Strips, 27

Liver Mousse Terrine with Almonds and Herbes de Provence, 134

Loin Chops with Fiddleheads, 104

Lunchtime Ham and Vegetable Salad, 61

Marinated Shrimp and Pork Kabobs, 77

Mexican Pork Tacos, 223

Minestrone with Pork Strips, 220

Mini-Sandwich on French Cheese Bread, 19

Okra and Baby Vegetable Soup, 219

Old Fashioned Cretons with Chives, 146

Old-Fashioned Pigs' Tails, 165

Oven-Baked Spareribs, 93

Panini with Parmesan and Balsamic Vinegar, 129

Pasta Salad with Mushrooms and Pork Strips, 53

Pâté de Campagne with Prunes, 125

Paupiettes à la Forestière, 185

Pears Stuffed with Ground Pork, 194

Pepper-Stuffed Cutlets, 85

Pickled Pork Cubes, 153

Pigs' Feet with Spicy Vinaigrette, 23

Pork and Mozzarella Pizza, 69

Pork and Parsley-Stuffed Pumpkin with Orange Sauce, 186

Pork, Cheese and Sun-Dried Tomato Sausages, 170

Pork Chops with Citrus Apricot Stuffing, 178

Pork Cubes Casserole with Beer and Celery, 141

Pork Cutlets with Avocado and Spinach, 82

Pork Hocks and Vegetables, 138

Pork Loin Stuffed with Herbes de Provence, 103

Pork Medallions and Ground Pork with Roasted Onions, 70

Pork Mini-Sausages with Beer and Onions, 145

Pork Pâté Au Jus, 54

Pork Pâté with Apples and Pumpkin, 57

Pork Roast and Bocconcini Sandwiches, 133

Pork Roast with Red Kidney Beans, 215

Pork Sauté à la Martiniquaise, 212

Pork Shepherd's Pie, 158

Pork Strips and Swiss Chard, 49

Pork Strips, Cauliflower and Vegetable Salad, 24

Pork Strips Salad with Avocados and Watercress, 126

Pork-Stuffed Vegetables, 193

Potatoes Stuffed with Pork and Cheddar, 58

Rack of Pork with Creamy Garlic, 99

Roast Pork Slices with Chinese Black Mushrooms, 224

Roasted Mini-Crown of Pork with Cranberry Sauce, 112

Sausage Patties with Pink Pepper, 161

Sautéed Marinated Pork with Zucchini Balls, 116

Shoulder Roast with Pumpkin and Pineapple Sauce, 149

Small Medallions with Sesame Seeds, 90

Small Pasta Shells with Pork Filling, 181

Small Slices of Cold Roast, with Coconut Vinaigrette, 20

Smoked Ham En Croûte, 154

Spaghetti with Pork Meat Sauce, 65

Spareribs with Sun-Dried Tomatoes, 108

Spicy Pork Kabobs with Puff Pastry, 74

Stuffed Liver, 182

Tenderloin Medallions with Summer Fruit, 111

Tenderloin Stuffed with Greens and Chives, 89

Tenderloin Stuffed with Peaches, 86

Three-Hour Braised Pork Roast, 169

Warm Pan-Fried Loin Chops and Tomatoes, 16

Winter Potato and Pork Stew, 166

Yellow and Red Peppers with Fresh Thyme Stuffing, 198

Zucchini Blossoms with Ricotta and Sun-Dried Tomato Filling, 190

3 1191 00563 0363